STEP Ladder

STEP 2

(600-word Lev

不思議の国のアリス

Alice's Adventures in Wonderland

Lewis Carroll

ルイス・キャロル

はじめに

みなさんは英語で何ができるようになりたいですか。

外国人と自由にコミュニケーションしたい
インターネット上の英語のサイトや、ペーパーバック、英字新聞を辞書なしで読めるようになりたい
字幕なしで洋画を見たい
受験や就職で有利になりたい
海外で活躍したい……

英語の基礎的な力、とりわけ読解力をつけるのに大切なのは、楽しみながら多読することです。数多くの英文に触れることによって、英語の発想や表現になじみ、英語の力が自然に身についてきます。

そうは言っても、何から手をつけていいのかわからないということはないでしょうか。やさしそうだと思って、外国の絵本や子ども向けの洋書を買ってはみたものの、知らない単語や表現ばかりが出てきて、途中で読むのをあきらめた経験がある方もいらっしゃるのではありませんか。

おすすめしたいのは、学習者向けにやさしく書かれた本から始めて、自分のレベルに合わせて、少しずつ難しいものに移っていく読み方です。

本書《ステップラダー・シリーズ》は、使用する単語を限定した、やさしい英語で書かれている英文リーダーで、初心者レベルの方でも、無理なく最後まで読めるように工夫されています。

みなさんが、楽しみながら英語の力をステップアップできるようになっています。

特長と使い方

●特長●

ステップラダー・シリーズは、世界の古典や名作などを、使用する単語を限定して、やさしい表現に書き改めた、英語初級〜初中級者向けの英文リーダーです。見開きごとのあらすじや、すべての単語の意味が載ったワードリストなど、初心者レベルでも負担なく、英文が読めるように構成されています。無料音声ダウンロード付きですので、文字と音声の両面で読書を楽しむことができます。

ステップ	使用語彙数	対象レベル	英検	CEFR
STEP 1	300語	中学1年生程度	5級	A1
STEP 2	600語	中学2年生程度	4級	A1
STEP 3	900語	中学3年生程度	3級	A2

●使い方●

- 本文以外のパートはすべてヘルプです。できるだけ本文に集中して読みましょう。
- 日本語の語順に訳して読むと速く読むことができません。文の頭から順番に、意味のかたまりごとに理解するようにしましょう。
- すべてを100パーセント理解しようとせず、ところどころ想像で補うようにして、ストーリーに集中する方が、楽に楽しく読めます。
- 黙読する、音読する、音声に合わせて読む、音声だけを聞くなど、いろいろな読み方をしてみましょう。

●無料音声ダウンロード●

本書の朗読音声（MP3形式）を、下記URLとQRコードから無料でダウンロードすることができます。

www.ibcpub.co.jp/step_ladder/0680/

※PCや端末、ソフトウェアの操作・再生方法については、編集部ではお答えできません。製造元にお問い合わせいただくか、インターネットで検索するなどして解決してください。

●構成●

トラック番号
朗読音声の番号です。

語数表示
開いたページの単語数と、読んできた総単語数が確認できます。

2

01 **Down the Rabbit Hole**

Alice was getting sleepy. She was sitting under a tree with her sister. Her sister was reading a book, but it did not seem very interesting.

[1]Suddenly, Alice saw a white rabbit run by. It was saying, "Oh, dear! I'm late! I'm late!"

Alice did not think this was very strange. [2]But then the rabbit took a watch out of its pocket to look at the time. This was strange indeed! Alice jumped up and followed it.

The rabbit jumped down a rabbit hole, so Alice did too.

(88 [88] words)

アリスは、突然「遅刻だ！」と言いながらポケットから時計を出して走る白うさぎを見かけて、後を追いかけてうさぎの穴に飛び込みました。

Down the Rabbit Hole 3

◆ **KEYWORDS**

- □ **rabbit** [rǽbɪt]
- □ **hole** [hóul]
- □ **Alice** [ǽlɪs]
- □ **sleepy** [slíːpi]
- □ *get sleepy*
- □ **seem** [síːm]
- □ **suddenly** [sʌ́dənli]
- □ *run by*
- □ *take ~ out of one's pocket*
- □ **indeed** [indíːd]
- □ *jump up*
- □ *jump down*

◆ **KEY SENTENCES** (☞ p. 70)

[1] Suddenly, • Alice saw a white rabbit • run by.

[2] But • then • the rabbit took a watch • out of its pocket • to look at the time.

あらすじ
本文のおおまかな内容がわかります。

キーセンテンス
長い文や難しい表現の文を、意味単位に区切って紹介しています。表示のページに訳があります。

キーワード
使用語彙以外で使われている初出の単語、熟語のリストです。発音記号の読み方は次ページの表を参考にしてください。

キーワードについて

1. 語尾が規則変化する単語は原形、不規則変化語は本文で出てきた形を見出しにしています。

   例　studies/studying/studied → study
   goes/going → go
   went → went
   gone → gone

2. 熟語に含まれる所有格の人称代名詞(my, your, his/her, theirなど)は one's に、再帰代名詞(myself, yourselfなど)は oneself に置き換えています。

   例　do your best → do one's best
   enjoy myself → enjoy oneself

3. 熟語に含まれるbe動詞 (is, are, was, were)は原形のbeに置き換えています。

   例　was going to → be going to

発音記号表

●母音●

/ɑ/	h**o**t, l**o**t
/ɑː/	**ar**m, **ar**t, c**ar**, h**ar**d, m**ar**ch, p**ar**k, f**a**ther
/æ/	**a**sk, b**a**g, c**a**t, d**a**nce, h**a**nd, m**a**n, th**a**nk
/aɪ/	**i**ce, n**i**ce, r**i**ce, t**i**me, wh**i**te, b**uy**, **eye**, fl**y**
/aɪə^{r}/	f**ire**, t**ire**
/aʊ/	br**ow**n, d**ow**n, n**ow**, h**ou**se, m**ou**th, **ou**t
/aʊə^{r}/	fl**ower**, sh**ower**, t**ower**, **hour**
/e/	b**e**d, **e**gg, fr**ie**nd, h**ea**d, h**e**lp, l**e**tter, p**e**t, r**e**d
/eɪ/	c**a**ke, m**a**ke, f**a**ce, g**a**me, n**a**me, d**ay**, pl**ay**
/eə^{r}/	c**are**, ch**air**, h**air**
/ɪ/	b**i**g, f**i**sh, g**i**ve, l**i**sten, m**i**lk, p**i**nk, s**i**ng
/iː/	**ea**t, r**ea**d, sp**ea**k, gr**ee**n, m**ee**t, w**ee**k, p**eo**ple
/ɪə^{r}/	d**ear**, **ear**, n**ear**, y**ear**
/oʊ/	c**o**ld, g**o**, h**o**me, n**o**te, **o**ld, c**oa**t, kn**ow**
/ɔː/	**a**ll, b**a**ll, c**a**ll, t**a**lk, w**a**lk
/ɔː^{r}/	d**oor**, m**ore**, sh**or**t
/ɔɪ/	b**oy**, enj**oy**, t**oy**
/ʊ/	b**oo**k, c**oo**k, f**oo**t, g**oo**d, l**oo**k, p**u**t
/uː/	f**oo**d, r**oo**m, sch**oo**l, fr**ui**t, j**ui**ce
/ʊə^{r}/	p**ure**, s**ure**
/əː^{r}/	b**ir**d, g**ir**l, th**ir**d, l**ear**n, t**ur**n, w**or**k
/ʌ/	b**u**s, cl**u**b, j**u**mp, l**u**nch, r**u**n, l**o**ve, m**o**ther
/ə/	**a**bout, **o**'clock
/i/	eas**y**, mon**ey**, ver**y**

●子音●

/b/	**b**ag, **b**all, **b**ed, **b**ig, **b**ook, clu**b**, jo**b**
/d/	**d**esk, **d**og, **d**oor, col**d**, foo**d**, frien**d**
/f/	**f**ace, **f**inger, **f**ish, **f**ood, hal**f**, i**f**, lau**gh**
/g/	**g**ame, **g**irl, **g**o, **g**ood, bi**g**, do**g**, e**gg**
/h/	**h**air, **h**and, **h**appy, **h**ome, **h**ot
/j/	**y**ellow, **y**es, **y**oung
/k/	**c**a**k**e, **c**oo**k**, **k**ing, des**k**, loo**k**, mil**k**, pin**k**, tal**k**
/l/	**l**earn, **l**eg, **l**itt**l**e, **l**ook, anima**l**, gir**l**, schoo**l**
/m/	**m**ake, **m**other, **m**ovie, ho**m**e, na**m**e, roo**m**, ti**m**e
/n/	**kn**ow, **n**ame, **n**ight, **n**oo**n**, pe**n**, ru**n**, trai**n**
/p/	**p**ark, **p**encil, **p**et, **p**ink, ca**p**, hel**p**, jum**p**, sto**p**
/r/	**r**ead, **r**ed, **r**ice, **r**oom, **r**un, w**r**ite
/s/	**s**ay, **s**ee, **s**ong, **s**tudy, **s**ummer, bu**s**, fa**c**e, i**c**e
/t/	**t**alk, **t**eacher, **t**ime, **t**rain, ca**t**, foo**t**, ha**t**, nigh**t**
/v/	**v**ery, **v**ideo, **v**isit, fi**v**e, gi**v**e, ha**v**e, lo**v**e, mo**v**ie
/w/	**w**alk, **w**ant, **w**eek, **w**oman, **w**ork
/z/	**z**ero, **z**oo, clothe**s**, ha**s**, mu**s**ic, no**s**e
/ʃ/	**sh**ip, **sh**ort, Engli**sh**, fi**sh**, sta**ti**on
/ʒ/	mea**s**ure, lei**s**ure, televi**s**ion
/ŋ/	ki**ng**, lo**ng**, si**ng**, spri**ng**, E**n**glish, dri**n**k, tha**n**k
/tʃ/	**ch**air, **ch**eap, ca**tch**, lun**ch**, mar**ch**, tea**ch**er, wa**tch**
/θ/	**th**ank, **th**ink, **th**ursday, bir**th**day, mon**th**, mou**th**, too**th**
/ð/	**th**ey, **th**is, **th**en, ba**th**e, bro**th**er, fa**th**er, mo**th**er
/dʒ/	**J**apan, **j**ump, **j**unior, bri**dg**e, chan**g**e, en**j**oy, oran**g**e

Table of Contents

『不思議の国のアリス』について

著者のルイス・キャロルは、本名をチャールズ・ラトウィッジ・ドジソンと言い、オックスフォード大学で数学の講師を務めていました。大学の学寮長ヘンリー・リデルの3人の幼い娘たちとピクニックに出かけて川で舟遊びをしているときに、次女アリスを主人公にして即興で語り聞かせた話が原型になっています。1865年に出版されて評判を呼んで以来、聖書やシェイクスピアに次ぐといわれるほど多くの言語に翻訳され、世界中で親しまれています。

■主なキャラクター

White Rabbit　白うさぎ　懐中時計を眺めて時間に追われている。実在した医学部の教授がモデルだと言われている

Mouse　ネズミ　アリスの涙のプールを泳ぎながら現れ、長い「尾話」を始める（尾tailと話taleは発音が同じ）

Mary Ann　メアリーアン　白うさぎがアリスと勘違いした召使の名。キャロルの友人の召使、メアリーアンという女性がモデルという説の他に、メアリーアンが当時、召使一般を指す語だったので、白うさぎがその場でアリスを召使扱いしたという説もある

Dodo　ドードー　レースを提案する。絶滅した鳥として当時から知られていた。吃音だったキャロル（ドジソン）自身を指している。どもるとき自分の名を「ド、ド、ドジソン」と発音したことから

Cheshire Cat　チェシャ猫　笑い顔をした猫。名前は「チェシャ猫のように笑う（grin like a Cheshire cat）」というキャロルの出生地チェシャー州で当時使われていた慣用表現から

Hatter　帽子屋　お茶会をしている。「帽子屋のように気が狂っている（as mad as a hatter）」という、当時の慣用表現から

Hare　うさぎ　お茶会をしている。「三月のうさぎのように気が狂っている（as mad as a March hare）」という、当時の慣用表現から

Queen of Hearts　ハートの女王　「首をはねろ！」が口癖の、傍若無人を絵に描いたような女王

Gryphon　グリフォン　アリスをにせウミガメのところへ連れて行く。伝説上の生物で体の上部は鷲、下部はライオン。オックスフォード大学トリニティ・カレッジの紋章に使われている

Mock Turtle　にせウミガメ　頭部が牛になったウミガメ。「にせウミガメのスープ」は実在した18世紀半ばのイギリス料理で、高価なウミガメの肉の代用として牛の頭部を使用した模造品

Alice's Adventures in Wonderland

不思議の国のアリス

01 Down the Rabbit Hole

Alice was getting sleepy. She was sitting under a tree with her sister. Her sister was reading a book, but it did not seem very interesting.

[1]Suddenly, Alice saw a White Rabbit run by. It was saying, "Oh, dear! I'm late! I'm late!"

Alice did not think this was very strange. [2]But then the Rabbit took a watch out of its pocket to look at the time. This was strange indeed! Alice jumped up and followed it.

The rabbit jumped down a rabbit hole, so Alice did too.

(88 [88] words)

アリスは、突然「遅刻だ！」と言いながらポケットから時計を出して走る白うさぎを見かけて、後を追いかけてうさぎの穴に飛び込みました。

◆ KEYWORDS

- ☐ **rabbit** [rǽbɪt]
- ☐ **hole** [hóʊl]
- ☐ **Alice** [ǽlɪs]
- ☐ **sleepy** [slíːpi]
- ☐ *get sleepy*
- ☐ **seem** [síːm]
- ☐ **suddenly** [sʌ́dənli]
- ☐ *run by*
- ☐ *take ~ out of one's pocket*
- ☐ **indeed** [ìndíːd]
- ☐ *jump up*
- ☐ *jump down*

◆ KEY SENTENCES (☞ p. 70)

1 Suddenly, • Alice saw a White Rabbit • run by.

2 But • then • the Rabbit took a watch • out of its pocket • to look at the time.

The hole was very deep and she fell straight down. She kept falling for a long time. Finally, she landed on some wood and leaves. She was not hurt.

A dark hallway was in front of her. She saw the Rabbit running down it. She ran after it, but it turned around a corner and disappeared.

3 Now she was in a hallway lined with doors. Alice tried every door, but they were all locked. She turned around and walked back.

4 To her surprise, she found a little table that wasn't there before. It had a little key on it.

Alice tried the key on all the doors but it didn't fit. Then, she saw a little curtain by the floor. Behind it was a little door.

うさぎを見失ったアリスは、カギが置かれたテーブルと廊下に並ぶドアに気がつきました。唯一カギが合った小さな扉の向こうには花園が見えました。

She got down and tried the key. It fit! She looked through the door to see a beautiful flower garden.

(146 [234] words)

◆ KEYWORDS

- ☐ **straight** [stréɪt]
- ☐ *fall straight down*
- ☐ **land** [lǽnd]
- ☐ **hurt** [hə́:ʳt]
- ☐ **dark** [dɑ́:ʳk]
- ☐ **hallway** [hɔ́:lwèɪ]
- ☐ *run after*
- ☐ **disappear** [dìsəpíəʳ]
- ☐ **line** [láɪn]
- ☐ *lined with*
- ☐ **lock** [lɑ́:k]
- ☐ **surprise** [səʳpráɪz]
- ☐ **fit** [fít]
- ☐ **curtain** [kə́:ʳtən]
- ☐ *get down*
- ☐ **garden** [gɑ́:ʳdən]

◆ KEY SENTENCES (☞ p. 70)

3 Now • she was in a hallway • lined with doors.

4 To her surprise, • she found a little table • that wasn't there • before.

Alice wanted to go into the garden, but she was much too big. She could not fit through the door.

Alice went back to the table. [5]She thought she might find something else useful on it. She did! There was a little bottle. It had the words "Drink Me" on it.

She was excited, but she was also a careful girl. [6]She looked for signs saying "dangerous" on it and found none. So she decided it was safe to drink.

It tasted nice, but she felt very strange.

"I must be getting smaller!" she said. And she was! She was shrinking every second. Finally, she was small enough to fit through the little door. She ran to the door, but she found that she forgot the key on the table! She began to cry.

ドアを通れないアリスは「私を飲んで」と書かれた小さなビンを見つけました。飲むと体が縮みましたが、カギを忘れてきたことに気づきました。

As she was crying, a little box appeared. It had the words "Eat Me" on it.

(150 [384] words)

◆ KEYWORDS

- ☐ *fit through the door*
- ☐ **might** [máɪt]
- ☐ *look for*
- ☐ **sign** [sáɪn]
- ☐ **decide** [dìsáɪd]
- ☐ **safe** [séɪf]
- ☐ *safe to drink*
- ☐ **taste** [téɪst]
- ☐ *every second*
- ☐ **shrink** [ʃríŋk]
- ☐ **enough** [ɪnʌ́f]
- ☐ **appear** [əpíə^r]

◆ KEY SENTENCES (☞ p. 70)

5 She thought • she might find something else • useful • on it.

6 She looked for signs • saying "dangerous" • on it • and found none.

02 The Pool of Tears

7 By now, Alice felt like none of these events were strange at all. She opened the box. Inside was a little cake. She ate it. She waited to see if she would grow smaller or bigger.

Suddenly, she found she was growing taller than the table and taller than the doors. When she stopped growing, she was nine feet tall! She was a giant! Now she would never get through the little door to the flower garden. This made her so sad that she cried giant tears.

8 Her tears were falling to the floor and making a pool all around her when she saw the White Rabbit again! He was carrying some beautiful white gloves and a fan.

(118 [502] words)

「私を食べて」と書かれた箱の中のケーキをアリスが食べると、今度は背が高くなり、扉を通れなくなったアリスは、悲しくて大粒の涙を流しました。

◆ KEYWORDS

- ☐ *by now*
- ☐ *at all*
- ☐ *see if*
- ☐ **tear** [tíəʳ]
- ☐ **giant** [dʒáɪənt]
- ☐ *get through*
- ☐ **never** [névəʳ]
- ☐ **sad** [sǽd]
- ☐ *so ~ that*
- ☐ **pool** [pú:l]
- ☐ **glove** [glʌ́v]

◆ KEY SENTENCES (☞ p. 70)

7 By now, • Alice felt like • none of these events were strange • at all.

8 Her tears were falling • to the floor • and making a pool • all around her • when she saw the White Rabbit • again!

"The Duchess! She will be so angry that I am late!" the White Rabbit was saying.

Alice wanted some help, so she said in a nice voice, "If you please, sir—"

But this surprised the rabbit. He jumped up, dropped his gloves and fan, and ran away.

Alice picked up the fan and gloves. Because it was very hot, she fanned herself as she spoke.

"How strange everything is today!" she said. "Everything was so normal yesterday. I wonder if I changed in the night. Maybe I've become somebody else. Maybe I've turned into my neighbor Mabel. [9]She is so different from me, for I know many things and Mabel—well, she

白うさぎを見てアリスが声をかけると、うさぎは手袋と扇子を落として逃げてしまいました。暑かったのでアリスは拾った扇子で自分をあおぎました。

knows very little. [10]I will see if I still know all the things I used to. Four times five is twelve, and four times six is thirteen."

(139 [641] words)

◆KEYWORDS

- ☐ **Duchess** [dʌ́tʃəs]
- ☐ **angry** [ǽŋgri]
- ☐ *if you please*
- ☐ **sir** [sə́ːʳ]
- ☐ **herself** [həʳsélf]
- ☐ **normal** [nɔ́ːʳməl]
- ☐ **wonder** [wʌ́ndəʳ]
- ☐ *wonder if*
- ☐ **somebody** [sʌ́mbədìː]
- ☐ *somebody else*
- ☐ *turn into*
- ☐ **neighbor** [néɪbəʳ]
- ☐ **Mabel** [méɪbəl]
- ☐ **still** [stíl]
- ☐ *used to*

◆KEY SENTENCES (☞ p. 70)

[9] She is so different from me, • for I know many things • and Mabel • —well, • she knows very little.

[10] I will see • if I still know • all the things • I used to.

That didn't sound very right.

"Oh, dear," said Alice. "Let me try something else. London is the capital of Paris, and Paris is the capital of Rome. No, that's wrong too. Oh, dear! I've turned into Mabel!"

[11]As she said this, she looked at herself and saw that she was growing small again.

She realized it was because she was fanning herself. She dropped the fan. She stopped shrinking. [12]But now she was so small that she was swimming in her own pool of giant tears!

"I wish I hadn't cried so much!" she said. She swam around and tried to find a way out. Just then, she saw a mouse swimming toward her.

アリスはとても小さくなって自分の流した涙のプールを泳いでいました。一匹のネズミが泳いできたので、アリスは出口がどこなのか尋ねました。

"Excuse me, Mouse!" said Alice. "Do you know the way out of this pool?"

(128 [769] words)

◆ KEYWORDS

- ☐ *Oh, dear!*
- ☐ **let** [lét]
- ☐ **London** [lʌ́ndən]
- ☐ **capital** [kǽpɪtəl]
- ☐ **Paris** [pǽrɪs]
- ☐ **Rome** [róʊm]
- ☐ **wrong** [rɔ́:ŋ]
- ☐ **realize** [rí:əlàɪz]
- ☐ **wish** [wíʃ]
- ☐ *I wish I hadn't done*
- ☐ *way out*
- ☐ *just then*
- ☐ **mouse** [máʊs]
- ☐ **toward** [təwɔ́:ʳd]

◆ KEY SENTENCES (☞ p. 70)

11 As she said this, • she looked at herself • and saw • that she was growing small • again.

12 But now • she was so small • that she was swimming • in her own pool • of giant tears!

The Mouse looked at her. He didn't seem to understand.

"Maybe it doesn't speak English," thought Alice. So she said in French, "Where is my cat?"

[13]At this, the Mouse jumped in fear and tried to swim away as fast as he could.

"Oh, I'm sorry!" Alice said. "[14]That was the first thing I learned how to say in French! I forgot that you don't like cats! Please come back."

The Mouse turned around and swam back to her. "Let's get out of the water," he said. "I will tell you my history. Then you will understand why I don't like cats."

Alice agreed. Now the water was filling

ネズミが英語を理解しないと思ったアリスはフランス語で「私の猫はどこ？」と言ってみました。ネズミは飛び上がり全力で逃げようとしました。

up with all kinds of animals—a Duck, a Dodo, an Eaglet, and other strange animals. So they all swam to shore.

(131 [900] words)

◆ KEYWORDS

- ☐ **French** [fréntʃ]
- ☐ **fear** [fíə^r]
- ☐ *in fear*
- ☐ *get out of*
- ☐ **agree** [əgríː]
- ☐ **fill** [fíl]
- ☐ *fill up with*
- ☐ **duck** [dʌ́k]
- ☐ **dodo** [dóʊdoʊ]
- ☐ **eaglet** [íːglɪt]
- ☐ **shore** [ʃɔ́ː^r]

◆ KEY SENTENCES (☞ p. 71)

[13] At this, • the Mouse jumped • in fear • and tried to swim away • as fast as he could.

[14] That was the first thing • I learned • how to say • in French!

03 A Caucus Race and a Long Story

They all sat in a square with the Mouse in the middle.

"I shall tell you a story," he said, "and the story will help you get dry."

15 So the Mouse began the story and they all listened, but they were not getting any drier. Alice pointed this out.

"Then we should have a caucus race!"
said the Dodo. He explained how to do it.
16 All the racers stood here and there along
a race course that was a strange shape.
Then, the racers ran or stopped whenever
they liked.

They tried it out. After they ran for about thirty minutes, the Dodo yelled, "Stop!"

(105 [1,005] words)

ネズミは話をすれば乾くと言いましたが、一向に乾きません。ドードーがレースを提案して、選手は奇妙な形のコースを走ったり止まったりしました。

◆ KEYWORDS

- ☐ **caucus** [kɔ́:kəs]
- ☐ **race** [réɪs]
- ☐ **square** [skwéə^{r}]
- ☐ **middle** [mídəl]
- ☐ *get dry*
- ☐ *not ~ any*
- ☐ *point out*
- ☐ **explain** [ɪkspléɪn]
- ☐ **racer** [réɪsə^{r}]
- ☐ **shape** [ʃéɪp]
- ☐ **whenever** [^{h}wenévə^{r}]
- ☐ *try out*
- ☐ **yell** [jél]

◆ KEY SENTENCES (☞ p. 71)

15 So the Mouse began the story • and they all listened, • but they were not getting any drier.

16 All the racers stood • here and there • along a race course • that was a strange shape.

Nobody knew who won. So the Dodo said they all won and they would all get prizes.

They all looked to Alice for their prizes. Alice took out a box of sweets from her pocket. She gave one to each animal.

They all cheered and ate their sweets. When they finished, they asked the Mouse to tell another story.

17 “You said you would tell me about why you don’t like cats,” said Alice.

“My story is long and sad!” said the Mouse. He started to tell it. But he stopped and walked away because he thought nobody was listening.

“Come back!” cried Alice. He kept walking.

全員がレースに勝ったと言われ、アリスは皆にお菓子を1つずつ与えました。その後、猫のダイナの話をするとアリスは一人きりになってしまいました。

[18]"I wish Dinah were here," said Alice. "She's my cat. She would know how to get the Mouse back. She is such a good hunter! She catches birds too."

All the birds jumped up and said they had to go. Now Alice was all alone.

(151 [1,156] words)

◆KEYWORDS

- ☐ **prize** [práɪz]
- ☐ *take out*
- ☐ **sweet** [swíːt]
- ☐ **cheer** [tʃíəʳ]
- ☐ **Dinah** [dáɪnə]
- ☐ **hunter** [hʌ́ntəʳ]

◆KEY SENTENCES (☞ p. 71)

[17] "You said • you would tell me • about why you don't like cats," • said Alice.

[18] "I wish • Dinah were here," • said Alice.

04 The Rabbit Needs Help

Alice was feeling very lonely. But she heard someone walking toward her. It was the White Rabbit again! He was looking for something.

As soon as he saw Alice, he shouted at her, "Mary Ann! What are you doing here? Run home and bring me my white gloves and fan! I've lost my others."

[19]Alice ran in the direction the White Rabbit was pointing to. Soon, she came to a house. It said "W. Rabbit" on the door. She went inside and found another pair of gloves and a fan on a table.

[20]She was just about to take them back to the Rabbit when she saw a little bottle.

白うさぎが現れ、アリスを見ると彼女に扇子と手袋を取ってくるように命じました。うさぎが指差す先の一軒家でアリスは小さなビンを見つけました。

She thought something interesting might happen if she drank it.

(120 [1,276] words)

◆KEYWORDS

- ☐ **lonely** [lóʊnli]
- ☐ *as soon as*
- ☐ **Mary Ann** [méri ǽn]
- ☐ **direction** [dɪrékʃən]
- ☐ **pair** [péə^{r}]
- ☐ *be about to*

◆KEY SENTENCES (☞ p. 71)

19 Alice ran • in the direction • the White Rabbit was pointing to.

20 She was just about • to take them back • to the Rabbit • when she saw a little bottle.

As soon as Alice drank from the bottle, she began to grow. Soon, her body took up the whole house!

Her head pushed against the ceiling.
21 She put her foot out the door and her arm through the window. Now Alice was really in trouble. How would she get out of the house?

Just then, she heard the White Rabbit's voice outside.

"There's a giant in my house! Help! Help!"

Alice listened. It sounded like more animals were coming. Then, they started throwing stones at her. One of the stones came in through the door. Alice realized they were small, hard cakes. So she took a bite.

アリスは巨大化して家からはみ出るほどになりましたが、動物たちが投げ込んだお菓子を食べると縮んだので、家を出て森の中まで走って逃げました。

She grew small again and ran outside.
22 The animals started to chase her but she ran until she was safe in a forest.

(130 [1,406] words)

◆KEYWORDS

- ☐ *take up*
- ☐ **whole** [hóʊl]
- ☐ **against** [əgénst]
- ☐ *push against*
- ☐ **ceiling** [síːlɪŋ]
- ☐ *put out*
- ☐ **trouble** [trʌ́bəl]
- ☐ *in trouble*
- ☐ **outside** [áʊtsáɪd]
- ☐ **throw** [θróʊ]
- ☐ **stone** [stóʊn]
- ☐ **bite** [báɪt]
- ☐ *take a bite*
- ☐ **chase** [tʃéɪs]
- ☐ **forest** [fɔ́ːrəst]

◆KEY SENTENCES (☞ p. 71)

[21] She put her foot • out the door • and her arm • through the window.

[22] The animals started to chase her • but she ran • until she was safe • in a forest.

05 A Caterpillar Helps

[23]Alice walked through the forest not knowing what to do. Now she was only three inches tall. She came to a large mushroom. A caterpillar sat on top of it, smoking.

"Who are you?" he asked.

"I'm not sure," answered Alice. "[24]I knew who I was yesterday, but today I don't know."

"What does that mean? Explain!" he said.

Alice tried to explain, but she got very confused.

"Who are you?" the Caterpillar asked again. "Or who do you want to be?"

(182 [1,488] words)

身長3インチのアリスは森の中でキノコの上に座ったイモムシに出会いました。イモムシに「あなたは誰？」と聞かれアリスは混乱してしまいました。

◆ KEYWORDS

- ☐ **caterpillar** [kǽtəpìləʳ]
- ☐ **inch** [íntʃ]
- ☐ **mushroom** [mʌ́ʃruːm]
- ☐ **smoke** [smóʊk]
- ☐ **confused** [kənfjúːzd]
- ☐ *get confused*
- ☐ *want to be*

◆ KEY SENTENCES (☞ p. 71)

23 Alice walked through the forest • not knowing • what to do.

24 I knew • who I was • yesterday, • but today • I don't know.

"I think I would like to be somebody bigger," Alice said.

"Have some of this mushroom. One side makes you smaller. The other side makes you bigger." Saying this, the Caterpillar vanished in a cloud of smoke.

Alice took some mushroom from each side. She took a bite of one and it made her as small as an ant. She ate some of the other and her neck grew so long that her head was taller than the trees.

[25]She ate a little of each piece until she was finally her usual size. She felt much better. She decided to go look for the beautiful flower garden. She walked through the forest until she came to a house.

キノコの両側を食べて元の大きさに戻ったアリスが森の中を歩くと家があり、その前でカエルの召使が女王から公爵夫人への手紙を読み上げました。

There was a frog standing outside of it. He was a servant. [26]He was opening a letter that was being delivered by a fish.

The frog read the letter out loud: "The Queen invites the Duchess to play croquet today."

This was very interesting to Alice, so she spoke to the frog.

(170 [1,658] words)

◆KEYWORDS

- ☐ **side** [sáɪd]
- ☐ **vanish** [vǽnɪʃ]
- ☐ **cloud** [kláʊd]
- ☐ **ant** [ǽnt]
- ☐ **piece** [píːs]
- ☐ **usual** [júːʒuːəl]
- ☐ **frog** [frɑ́ːg]
- ☐ **servant** [sə́ːʳvənt]
- ☐ **deliver** [dɪlívəʳ]
- ☐ *out loud*
- ☐ **queen** [kwíːn]
- ☐ **invite** [ìnváɪt]
- ☐ **croquet** [kroʊkéɪ]

◆KEY SENTENCES (☞ p. 71–72)

[25]She ate • a little of each piece • until she was • finally • her usual size.

[26]He was opening a letter • that was being delivered • by a fish.

06 Pig and Pepper

27 The frog didn't answer any of Alice's questions in a sensible way. So Alice decided to go into the house instead.

Inside was a strange sight. The Duchess was sitting in a chair holding a crying baby. The cook was making soup. But there was too much pepper in the air. Everybody was sneezing. Sometimes, the cook threw plates right at the Duchess and the baby!

"Oh, please be careful!" Alice said to the cook. But the cook kept throwing plates.

"Here!" said the Duchess, seeing Alice. "You hold the baby."

アリスが家に入ると、コックが赤ちゃんを抱く公爵夫人に皿を投げつけていました。赤ちゃんを連れて家を出たアリスが見ると、赤ちゃんは豚でした。

The baby was screaming loudly. [28]Alice ran out of the house with the baby to keep it safe. But when she finally looked down at it, she saw that it was not a baby at all. It was a pig.

(131 [1,789] words)

◆KEYWORDS

- ☐ **pepper** [pépəʳ]
- ☐ **sensible** [sénsəbəl]
- ☐ *in a sensible way*
- ☐ **instead** [ìnstéd]
- ☐ **sight** [sáɪt]
- ☐ **soup** [sú:p]
- ☐ **air** [éəʳ]
- ☐ **sneeze** [sní:z]
- ☐ **threw** [θrú:] < throw
- ☐ *throw ~ at*
- ☐ **plate** [pléɪt]
- ☐ **scream** [skrí:m]
- ☐ *keep ~ safe*

◆KEY SENTENCES (☞ p. 72)

[27]The frog didn't answer • any of Alice's questions • in a sensible way.

[28]Alice ran out of the house • with the baby • to keep it safe.

Alice put the pig down on the ground. It stopped screaming and went off very happily into the woods.

"It was not a very pretty baby, but it was a very nice-looking pig," said Alice.

29 Now she did not know what to do so she walked through the forest until she came to a cat sitting in a tree. It was grinning very wide.

"Hello," said Alice. "I didn't know cats could grin."

"I'm a Cheshire Cat. We always grin."

"I see. Could you please tell me which way to go?"

"A Hatter lives that way," said the Cat, pointing. "And a Hare lives that way. But

アリスは木の上で笑うチェシャ猫に会いました。道を尋ねると「帽子屋はあっち、うさぎはそっち。でも皆狂っているよ」と言って消えていきました。

they are all crazy. We are all crazy here. You are too."

[30]Alice thanked the Cheshire Cat for the directions. The Cat just grinned and disappeared.

(133 [1,922] words)

◆KEYWORDS

- ☐ *go off*
- ☐ **nice-looking** [nàɪslʊ́kɪŋ]
- ☐ **grin** [grín]
- ☐ **wide** [wáɪd]
- ☐ **Cheshire Cat** [tʃéʃəʳ kǽt]
- ☐ **hatter** [hǽtəʳ]
- ☐ *that way*
- ☐ **hare** [héəʳ]
- ☐ **crazy** [kréɪzi]

◆KEY SENTENCES (☞ p. 72)

[29]Now • she did not know • what to do • so she walked through the forest • until she came to a cat • sitting in a tree.

[30]Alice thanked the Cheshire Cat • for the directions.

07 The Tea Party

Alice walked to the Hare's house. She found the Hare and Hatter sitting at a large table. [31]The table was set with many cups for a tea party. A mouse was also there, but it was asleep. Alice also sat down at the table.

[32]"Putting butter in my broken watch did not fix it," said the Hatter to the Hare.

"But it was the best butter," said the Hare.

"Butter doesn't fix watches," said Alice.

"How do we fix broken time?" asked the Hare.

"Let's change places. I want a new cup," said the Hatter.

(95 [2,017] words)

うさぎの家に行くとうさぎと帽子屋と眠りネズミがお茶会をしていました。帽子屋は「壊れた時計にバターを入れたが直らないんだ」と言いました。

◆ KEYWORDS

- ☐ **set** [sét]
- ☐ **asleep** [əslíːp]
- ☐ **butter** [bʌ́tər]
- ☐ **broken** [bróʊkən]
- ☐ **fix** [fíks]
- ☐ **place** [pléɪs]
- ☐ *change places*

◆ KEY SENTENCES (☞ p. 72)

31 The table was set • with many cups • for a tea party.

32 "Putting butter • in my broken watch • did not fix it," • said the Hatter • to the Hare.

[33]They all got up and moved over one seat to where there was a new tea cup.

“Oh, dear. The Cheshire Cat was right. This Hare and Hatter seem to be very crazy,” Alice thought.

The Hare, Hatter, and the sleeping mouse continued to talk nonsense. Alice couldn’t stand it anymore. She rushed out of the tea party.

She walked through the forest until she came to a tree with a door in it. When she went inside, she was back in the hallway with the table and the door to the beautiful flower garden.

“This time, I know what to do!” said Alice.

お茶会を抜け出し森の中を歩いてドアのある木にたどり着いたアリスが、ちょうどいい大きさになってドアを通るとそこにバラ園が広がっていました。

34 She ate some mushroom until she was the right size to pick up the little golden key on the table. Then she ate the other mushroom until she was small enough to walk through the door.

She opened the door and went through to a beautiful rose garden.

(152 [2,169] words)

◆ KEYWORDS

☐ *get up*
☐ *move over*
☐ **seat** [síːt]
☐ **continue** [kəntínjuː]
☐ **nonsense** [nάːnsens]
☐ **golden** [góʊldən]
☐ **rose** [róʊz]

◆ KEY SENTENCES (☞ p. 72)

33 They all got up • and moved over one seat • to where • there was a new tea cup.

34 She ate some mushroom • until she was the right size • to pick up the little golden key • on the table.

08 The Queen's Croquet Ground

35 In the rose garden, three playing cards were painting a tree of white roses red.

"Excuse me, but why are you painting those roses?" Alice asked.

"It's supposed to be a tree of red roses. If the Queen knew it was white, she would cut off our heads," said one of the playing cards.

"How terrible!" said Alice.

Just then, the King of Hearts, the Queen of Hearts, and their court came through the garden. The Queen noticed Alice.

"Who are you?" demanded the Queen.

3人のトランプのカードが白いバラを赤く塗っていました。そこへハートの王と女王たち一行がやってきて、アリスに「おまえは誰か」と尋ねました。

"My name is Alice." Alice felt strong.
36 She knew they were just playing cards and she was not afraid of them.

(106 [2,275] words)

◆ KEYWORDS

- ☐ *playing card*
- ☐ **suppose** [səpóʊz]
- ☐ *be supposed to*
- ☐ *cut off someone's head*
- ☐ **heart** [hɑ́ːʳt]
- ☐ **court** [kɔ́ːʳt]
- ☐ *come through*
- ☐ **notice** [nóʊtɪs]
- ☐ **demand** [dɪmǽnd]
- ☐ *afraid of*

◆ KEY SENTENCES (☞ p. 72)

35 In the rose garden, • three playing cards were painting • a tree of white roses • red.

36 She knew • they were just playing cards • and she was not afraid of them.

[37]The Queen saw the three playing cards and a white rose that was half painted.

"Off with their heads!" she cried.

The Queen turned to Alice again.

"Can you play croquet?" she shouted.

"Yes!" Alice shouted back.

"Come on then!" cried the Queen.

Just then the White Rabbit came up to Alice and said in a quiet voice, "It's a fine day today."

"It is," said Alice. "Where is the Duchess? Wasn't she invited to play croquet?"

[38]"The Queen has ordered her head to be cut off," said the White Rabbit.

(91 [2,366] words)

女王はバラを見て「彼らの首を切れ！」と叫び、その後アリスをクロッケーに誘いました。白うさぎがきたのでアリスは公爵夫人について尋ねました。

◆KEYWORDS

- ☐ **half** [hǽf]
- ☐ *Off with someone's head!*
- ☐ *come up to*
- ☐ **invite** [ìnváɪt]
- ☐ **order** [ɔ́ːʳdəʳ]

◆KEY SENTENCES (☞ p. 72)

37 The Queen saw the three playing cards • and a white rose • that was half painted.

38 "The Queen has ordered • her head • to be cut off," • said the White Rabbit.

"Go to your places!" the Queen shouted very loudly. Everybody started running here and there. The game began in a few minutes.

[39]Alice thought it was the strangest croquet ground she had ever seen. The balls were hedgehogs. The mallets were flamingoes. The arches were playing cards, standing on their hands and feet.

The main problem Alice had was holding her flamingo. Alice had to hold its thin legs under her arm. Then she put its long neck toward the ground. Its head was supposed to hit the ball. [40]But when she got the flamingo in position, it always moved and looked up into her face. This made Alice laugh. Meanwhile, the hedgehog would move away. All in all, it was a very difficult game.

奇妙なクロッケー場でした。ボールはハリネズミでマレットはフラミンゴです。女王はとても怒っていて「首を切れ！」と叫んで回っていました。

None of the players took turns and everybody seemed angry at each other. The Queen was very angry and went around shouting, "Off with his head! Off with her head!"

(155 [2,521] words)

◆ KEYWORDS

- ☐ **ever** [évəʳ]
- ☐ **seen** [síːn]
- ☐ **hedgehog** [hédʒhɑ̀ːg]
- ☐ **mallet** [mǽlɪt]
- ☐ **flamingo** [fləmíŋgoʊ]
- ☐ **arch** [ɑ́ːʳtʃ]
- ☐ **main** [méɪn]
- ☐ **thin** [θín]
- ☐ **position** [pəzíʃən]
- ☐ *get ~ in position*
- ☐ *make someone laugh*
- ☐ **meanwhile** [míːnwàɪl]
- ☐ *all in all*
- ☐ **player** [pléɪəʳ]
- ☐ *take turns*
- ☐ **seem** [síːm]

◆ KEY SENTENCES (☞ p. 73)

39 Alice thought • it was the strangest croquet ground • she had ever seen.

40 But • when she got the flamingo • in position, • it always moved • and looked up • into her face.

Alice began to feel worried. [41]She had not had any problems with the Queen, but it could happen any time. Alice worried she might be killed.

"They really like killing people here," thought Alice. "It's surprising that anybody is still alive."

Alice thought about running away. But then she noticed the smile of the Cheshire Cat.

"How are you getting on?" said the Cat.

Alice told the Cat everything that was going on. Then she noticed the King and Queen were listening to her.

The King demanded that the Cat kiss his hand. When the Cat refused, the Queen declared, "Off with his head!"

アリスが逃げだそうと思ったときチェシャ猫に気づきました。アリスがフラミンゴを探して戻ってくると、ハリネズミはまたいなくなっていました。

The King hurried off to find the Executioner. Alice went back to the game to look for her hedgehog.

Alice's hedgehog was fighting with another hedgehog. [42]She hurried to find her flamingo, but when she came back, the hedgehog was gone again.

(146 [2,667] words)

◆KEYWORDS

- ☐ **kill** [kíl]
- ☐ **surprising** [səʳpráɪzɪŋ]
- ☐ **anybody** [éni:bədi]
- ☐ **alive** [əláɪv]
- ☐ *How are you getting on?*
- ☐ **kiss** [kís]
- ☐ **refuse** [rɪfjú:z]
- ☐ **declare** [dɪkléəʳ]
- ☐ *hurry off*
- ☐ **executioner** [èksəkjú:ʃənəʳ]
- ☐ **hurry** [hə́:ri]
- ☐ **gone** [gɔ́:n]

◆KEY SENTENCES (☞ p. 73)

[41] She had not had any problems • with the Queen, • but it could happen • any time.

[42] She hurried • to find her flamingo, • but when she came back, • the hedgehog was gone • again.

[43]"But it doesn't matter much," thought Alice, "because the cards who are making the arches have left as well." She went back to talk to her friend the Cat.

The Cat was surrounded by a large group. The Executioner said he could not cut off the head because the Cat had no body. The King disagreed. The Queen said if something did not happen soon, she would have everyone's head cut off.

Alice said, "The Cat belongs to the Duchess. We can ask her."

The Executioner was sent to get the Duchess out of prison. [44]But the Cat disappeared by the time he came back with the Duchess. So everyone started to play croquet again.

(155 [2,782] words)

猫は体がなかったので処刑人は首を切れません。処刑人が公爵夫人を連れて戻ってくると猫は消えていたので、みんなはクロッケーを再開しました。

◆ KEYWORDS

- ☐ **matter** [mǽtəʳ]
- ☐ *as well*
- ☐ **surround** [səráʊnd]
- ☐ **disagree** [dɪsəgríː]
- ☐ **belong** [bɪlɔ́ːŋ]
- ☐ *belong to*
- ☐ **prison** [prízən]
- ☐ **disappear** [dìsəpíəʳ]
- ☐ *by the time*

◆ KEY SENTENCES (☞ p. 73)

43 "But it doesn't matter much," • thought Alice, • "because the cards • who are making the arches • have left • as well."

44 But the Cat disappeared • by the time • he came back • with the Duchess.

09 The Mock Turtle's Story

"I am very glad to see you again, you dear old thing!" said the Duchess to Alice. She put her arm into Alice's.

Alice was surprised and happy to find the Duchess so friendly. [45]She thought to herself that maybe it was only the pepper that had made the Duchess so angry when they met in the kitchen.

"Maybe it is always pepper that makes people angry," Alice thought to herself.

The Duchess began to rest her head on Alice's shoulder. [46]Alice did not like it, but she wanted to be polite so she did not protest. Alice began to talk about the croquet game.

公爵夫人に「また会えてうれしい」と言われてアリスはうれしくなりましたが、公爵夫人はまだ自分の首を切ろうとしている女王を見て逃げ出しました。

Suddenly, the Duchess began shaking with fear. Alice looked up and saw the Queen looking very, very angry.

The Duchess ran off, because the Queen still wanted to cut her head off.

(137 [2,919] words)

◆KEYWORDS

- □ **mock** [mɑ́:k]
- □ **turtle** [tə́:ʳtəl]
- □ *old thing*
- □ *think to oneself*
- □ **rest** [rést]
- □ **shoulder** [ʃóʊldəʳ]
- □ **protest** [prətést]
- □ **shake** [ʃéɪk]

◆KEY SENTENCES (☞ p. 73)

45 She thought to herself • that maybe • it was only the pepper • that had made the Duchess • so angry • when they met • in the kitchen.

46 Alice did not like it, • but she wanted to be polite • so she did not protest.

Everyone returned to the croquet game. After a while, the Queen got tired. She turned to Alice and asked, "Have you seen the Mock Turtle yet? He must tell you a story."

They walked until they saw a Gryphon lying asleep in the sun. The Queen ordered the Gryphon to take Alice to the Mock Turtle. [47]Then she left to make sure the Executioner was doing his job.

[48]Alice was worried, but the Gryphon laughed and told Alice that no one actually had their heads cut off. They set off to find the Mock Turtle. After a while, they saw the Mock Turtle sitting alone on a small rock, crying.

"This young lady," said the Gryphon, "wants to know your history."

女王に言われて、アリスはグリフォンと一緒ににせウミガメに会いました。
にせウミガメは「昔、僕は本物のカメだったんだ」と言って泣き始めました。

They sat silently until finally the Mock Turtle said, "Once, I was a real turtle." Then he began crying again.

(141 [3,060] words)

◆KEYWORDS

- ☐ **while** [^{h}wáɪl]
- ☐ *after a while*
- ☐ *get tired*
- ☐ **yet** [jét]
- ☐ **Gryphon** [gríf^{ə}n]
- ☐ **lying** [láɪɪŋ] < lie
- ☐ *no one*
- ☐ **actually** [ǽktʃùːəli]
- ☐ *set off*
- ☐ **lady** [léɪdi]
- ☐ **silently** [sáɪləntli]
- ☐ **once** [wʌ́ns]

◆KEY SENTENCES (☞ p. 73)

47 Then • she left to make sure • the Executioner was doing his job.

48 Alice was worried, • but the Gryphon laughed • and told Alice • that no one actually had their heads • cut off.

[49]At last the Mock Turtle said, "When we were little, we went to school by the sea, where we were taught by an old turtle called 'Tortoise.'"

After crying again, the Mock Turtle continued. [50]"We went to school every day and studied French, music, and washing—as well as the usual subjects like mathematics, reading, writing, and uglification."

"I've never heard of 'uglification,'" said Alice. "What is it?"

"Never heard of 'uglifying'!" the Gryphon cried. "Do you know what 'to beautify' is?"

Alice nodded.

"Good. Enough about lessons," said the Gryphon. "Tell her about the games now."

(97 [3,157] words)

にせウミガメは学校で学んだことについて話し、アリスは聞いたことのない教科に驚きました。グリフォンはカメにゲームの話をするよう言いました。

◆KEYWORDS

- ☐ *at last*
- ☐ **tortoise** [tɔ́ːʳtəs]
- ☐ **music** [mjúːzɪk]
- ☐ *as well as*
- ☐ **mathematics** [mæ̀θəmǽtɪks]
- ☐ *hear of*
- ☐ **uglification** [ʌ̀glifɪkéɪʃən]
- ☐ **uglify** [ʌ́glifàɪ]
- ☐ **beautify** [bjúːtɪfàɪ]
- ☐ **nod** [nɑ́ːd]

◆KEY SENTENCES (☞ p. 74)

49 At last • the Mock Turtle said, • "When we were little, • we went to school • by the sea, • where we were taught • by an old turtle • called 'Tortoise.'"

50 "We went to school • every day • and studied French, music, and washing • —as well as the usual subjects • like mathematics, reading, writing, and uglification."

10 The Lobster-Quadrille

The Mock Turtle was crying again, so the Gryphon began shaking him. This seemed to help and the Mock Turtle began speaking.

[51]“Perhaps you have never met a lobster, so you have no idea what a wonderful dance a Lobster-Quadrille is!”

“No,” said Alice.

“Why,” said the Gryphon, “you must first make a line along the beach.”

“Two lines!” cried the Mock Turtle.

“That generally takes some time,” said the Gryphon. “Then you walk forward two steps...”

にせウミガメは『ロブスター・カドリール』がいかに素晴らしいダンスかわからないでしょうとアリスに言い、グリフォンと一緒に手順を説明しました。

[52]They went on to explain the steps of the dance in detail.

"It must be a pretty dance," said Alice.

(97 [3,254] words)

◆ KEYWORDS

- ☐ **Lobster-Quadrille** [lɑ́ːbstəʳ kwɑdríl]
- ☐ **perhaps** [pəʳhǽps]
- ☐ **lobster** [lɑ́ːbstəʳ]
- ☐ **generally** [dʒénərəli]
- ☐ *take some time*
- ☐ **forward** [fɔ́ːʳwəʳd]
- ☐ **step** [stép]
- ☐ *go on to*
- ☐ **detail** [díːteɪl]
- ☐ *in detail*

◆ KEY SENTENCES (☞ p. 74)

[51]"Perhaps • you have never met a lobster, • so you have no idea • what a wonderful dance • a Lobster-Quadrille is!"

[52]They went on • to explain • the steps of the dance • in detail.

"Would you like to see a little of it?" asked the Mock Turtle.

"Yes, very much," said Alice.

"Come, let us try the first part!" said the Mock Turtle.

So they began dancing around Alice. Meanwhile, the Mock Turtle sang a song, very slowly and sadly. It was a strange song, all about a whiting, a porpoise, and a snail.

When the song ended, Alice said, "Thank you, it's a very interesting dance." She was very happy that the song was over.

53 The Mock Turtle asked if Alice had ever seen a whiting.

"Oh, yes," Alice answered, "They have their tails in their mouths."

二人はアリスの周りを踊り始ました。にせウミガメはゆっくりと悲しげに歌を歌い、それからアリスにホワイティングを見たことがあるか尋ねました。

[54]The Mock Turtle closed his eyes, so the Gryphon explained that they got their tails stuck in their mouths while dancing with the lobsters at sea.

(130 [3,384] words)

◆KEYWORDS

- □ **slowly** [slóʊli]
- □ **sadly** [sǽdli]
- □ **whiting** [ʰwáɪtɪŋ]
- □ **porpoise** [pɔ́ːʳpəs]
- □ **snail** [snéɪl]
- □ *ask if*
- □ **tail** [téɪl]
- □ **stuck** [stʌ́k]

◆KEY SENTENCES (☞ p. 74)

[53]The Mock Turtle asked • if Alice had ever seen a whiting.

[54]The Mock Turtle closed his eyes, • so the Gryphon explained • that they got their tails stuck • in their mouths • while dancing with the lobsters • at sea.

Alice was becoming very confused, but luckily the Gryphon said, “Let’s hear some of your adventures.”

So Alice began telling them about her adventures. [55]As she talked, her listeners began standing very close to her, very quietly, with their mouths wide open. Alice continued until she got to the part about her talking to the Caterpillar.

“That’s very strange!” said the Mock Turtle.

Then they made Alice stand up and recite a poem called *It Is the Voice of the Lobster*. But they soon stopped her and suggested another Lobster-Quadrille. Alice was relieved.

二人はアリスに詩の朗読をさせ、にせウミガメが「カメのスープ」を歌い始めると、遠くで「裁判が始まるぞ！」という叫び声が聞こえてきました。

[56]The Mock Turtle began singing 'Turtle Soup,' although he had to take breaks to cry.

Suddenly, the song was interrupted by a cry of "The trial is beginning!" in the distance.

"Come on!" cried the Gryphon, and hurried off toward the trial with Alice.

(137 [3,521] words)

◆KEYWORDS

- □ **luckily** [lʌ́kəli]
- □ **adventure** [ædvéntʃər]
- □ **listener** [lísnər]
- □ *get to*
- □ **recite** [rəsáɪt]
- □ **suggest** [sədʒést]
- □ **relieved** [rɪlíːvd]
- □ **although** [ɔ̀ːlðóʊ]
- □ *take a break*
- □ **interrupt** [ìntərʌ́pt]
- □ **trial** [tráɪəl]
- □ **distance** [dístəns]
- □ *in the distance*

◆KEY SENTENCES (☞ p. 74)

[55]As she talked, • her listeners began standing • very close to her, • very quietly, • with their mouths wide open.

[56]The Mock Turtle began singing 'Turtle Soup,' • although he had to take breaks • to cry.

11 Who Stole the Tarts

When they arrived at the trial, they found the King acting as the Judge. Twelve small animals were the jurors. The Queen and the playing cards were also there, along with the White Rabbit. He yelled, "Quiet in the court!" to begin the trial.

[57]The White Rabbit said that the Knave of Hearts was accused of taking the Queen's tarts.

The first witness was the Hatter. He came in with a teacup in one hand and a piece of bread and butter in the other.

"Tell us what you know," said the King.
[58]"If you don't, I will have you killed." This made the Hatter nervous.

(106 [3,627] words)

王様が裁判官で、陪審員は小動物、女王と白うさぎもいました。ハートのジャックが女王のタルトを奪った罪で訴えられ、最初の証人は帽子屋でした。

◆ KEYWORDS

- ☐ **stole** [stóʊl] < steal
- ☐ **tart** [tɑ́:ʳt]
- ☐ **act** [ǽkt]
- ☐ *act as*
- ☐ **judge** [dʒʌ́dʒ]
- ☐ **juror** [dʒʊ́ərəʳ]
- ☐ *along with*
- ☐ **knave** [néɪv]
- ☐ **accuse** [əkjú:z]
- ☐ *accused of*
- ☐ **witness** [wítnəs]
- ☐ **teacup** [tí:kʌ̀p]
- ☐ *have someone kiilled*
- ☐ **nervous** [nə́:ʳvəs]

◆ KEY SENTENCES (☞ p. 74–75)

57 The White Rabbit said • that the Knave of Hearts was accused • of taking the Queen's tarts.

58 "If you don't, • I will have you killed."

Just then, Alice began to feel strange.

[59]Alice was beginning to grow larger again, but she decided to stay where she was as long as there was room.

As Alice grew, she began bumping into other people. They got up angrily to find other seats.

The Queen never stopped watching the Hatter. The Hatter was growing more nervous and wasn't making much sense.

"You're a very bad speaker," said the King. "You may go." The Hatter quickly left the Court.

"Call the next witness!" said the King.

Alice was interested to know who the next witness would be.

アリスは自分が再び大きくなり始めたのに気づきました。帽子屋のあまり意味のない証言のあと、次の証人として呼ばれたのはなんとアリスでした。

[60]Imagine her surprise when the White Rabbit read out the name, "Alice!"

(110 [3,737] words)

◆KEYWORDS

- ☐ *as long as*
- ☐ **bump** [bʌ́mp]
- ☐ *bump into*
- ☐ **angrily** [ǽŋgrəli]
- ☐ **seat** [síːt]
- ☐ **sense** [séns]
- ☐ *make much sense*
- ☐ **bad** [bǽd]
- ☐ **speaker** [spíːkəʳ]
- ☐ **quickly** [kwíkli]
- ☐ **imagine** [ìmǽdʒən]
- ☐ *read out*

◆KEY SENTENCES (☞ p. 75)

[59]Alice was beginning to grow larger • again, • but she decided to stay • where she was • as long as there was room.

[60]Imagine her surprise • when the White Rabbit read out the name, • "Alice!"

12 Alice's Evidence

"Here!" cried Alice. She jumped up but she forgot how large she was now. [61]She bumped into the jury box, knocking all of the animals over.

[62]When the jurors were sitting again, the King asked Alice, "What do you know about this business?"

"Nothing," Alice answered.

"That's very important," said the King. All of the jurors began taking notes.

Suddenly, the King called out, "Silence!" He read out from his book, "Rule forty two. All persons more than a mile high are to leave the court."

アリスは「何も知らない」と答え、王様のアリスを追い出す新ルールの動議は白うさぎに邪魔されました。ジャックが書いた手紙が見つかったのです。

Alice protested this new rule, but she was interrupted by the White Rabbit. He said, "There's more for the jurors to hear. I have just picked up a letter written by the Knave."

(118 [3,855] words)

◆ **KEYWORDS**

- ☐ **evidence** [évədəns]
- ☐ **jury** [dʒʊ́əri]
- ☐ *jury box*
- ☐ **knock** [nɑ́:k]
- ☐ **business** [bíznəs]
- ☐ **note** [nóʊt]
- ☐ *take notes*
- ☐ *call out*
- ☐ **silence** [sáɪləns]
- ☐ **mile** [máɪl]
- ☐ *pick up*
- ☐ **written** [rítən] < write

◆ **KEY SENTENCES** (☞ p. 75)

61 She bumped into the jury box, • knocking all of the animals over.

62 When the jurors were sitting • again, • the King asked Alice, • "What do you know • about this business?"

The White Rabbit opened the paper and said, “Actually, it isn’t a letter. It’s a poem.”

“Is it in the Knave’s handwriting?” asked a juror.

“No, it’s not,” said the White Rabbit, “and that is the strangest thing about it.”

“Please, sir,” said the Knave, “I didn’t write any poem.”

[63]The Queen was ready to have the Knave’s head cut off. But Alice asked what was written on the paper.

“Read it!” said the King.

The White Rabbit read the poem. It was very confusing and did not make much sense at all.

内容は手紙ではなく詩で、ジャックは書いていないと言いました。王様の命令で白うさぎが詩を読みましたが、まったく意味をなしていませんでした。

Alice, the Knave, the King, and the Queen spent some time discussing the poem. They tried to make sense of it.

[64]"Let the jury tell us what they think," the King said.

(125 [3,980] words)

◆ **KEYWORDS**

☐ **poem** [póʊəm]
☐ **handwriting** [hǽndràɪtɪŋ]
☐ **confusing** [kənfjú:ziŋ]
☐ **discuss** [dɪskʌ́s]
☐ *make sense of*

◆ **KEY SENTENCES** (☞ p. 75)

[63]The Queen was ready • to have the Knave's head cut off.

[64]"Let the jury tell us • what they think," • the King said.

“No, no!” said the Queen. [65]“The jurors can tell us what they think after we have decided what to do with the Knave.”

“No, they can’t!” said Alice loudly. (Now she was so large that she wasn’t afraid of speaking.)

“Cut off her head!” the Queen shouted. Nobody moved.

“Who cares about you?” said Alice (she was her full size now). “You’re nothing but a bunch of cards!”

All of the cards started to rush toward Alice. She gave a little cry and tried to get away. [66]But she suddenly found herself lying by the river with her head on her sister’s leg.

(103 [4,083] words)

すっかり大きくなって何も恐れなくなったアリスが「あなたたちなんかただのカードの束よ！」と言うと、すべてのカードがアリスに突進してきました。

◆KEYWORDS

☐ *nothing but*
☐ **bunch** [bʌ́ntʃ]
☐ *rush toward*

◆KEY SENTENCES (☞ p. 75)

65 "The jurors can tell us • what they think • after we have decided • what to do • with the Knave."

66 But she suddenly found herself • lying by the river • with her head on her sister's leg.

"Wake up, Alice!" said her sister.

"Oh, I had such a strange dream!" said Alice. She told her sister as much as she could remember.

After sharing her story, Alice went back to her house to have her tea.

Alice's sister stayed by the river and soon she too began dreaming all about the White Rabbit, the Hatter, the Gryphon, and the terrible Queen.

She sat with closed eyes and imagined that she was in Wonderland. But she knew that if she opened her eyes again, everything would change back to reality.

67 Finally, she imagined Alice all grown up and how she would keep her simple, child's heart.

アリスはお姉さんに見ていた夢のことを話しました。お姉さんはアリスが大人になっても子どものような素朴な心を持ち続けることを想像しました。

[68]Maybe she would tell her own children about her happy summer days as a child, and about her dream of Wonderland long ago.

(131 [4,214] words)

◆**KEYWORDS**

☐ **wake** [wéɪk]
☐ **remember** [rɪmémbəʳ]
☐ **reality** [rì:ǽlətì:]
☐ *grown up*
☐ **simple** [símpəl]
☐ **wonderland** [wʌ́ndəʳlæ̀nd]
☐ *long ago*

◆**KEY SENTENCES** (☞ p. 75)

[67]Finally, • she imagined Alice all grown up • and how she would keep • her simple, • child's heart.

[68]Maybe • she would tell her own children • about her happy summer days • as a child, • and about her dream • of Wonderland • long ago.

〈 KEY SENTENCES の訳 〉

1. Suddenly, Alice saw a White Rabbit run by.
突然、アリスは白いうさぎが走ってくるのを見ました。

2. But then the Rabbit took a watch out of its pocket to look at the time.
しかし、それからうさぎはポケットから時計を取り出して時間を見ました。

3. Now she was in a hallway lined with doors.
今、彼女はドアの並んだ廊下にいました。

4. To her surprise, she found a little table that wasn't there before.
驚いたことに、彼女は以前にはなかった小さなテーブルを見つけました。

5. She thought she might find something else useful on it.
彼女は何か役に立つ他のものが見つかるかもしれないと思いました。

6. She looked for signs saying "dangerous" on it and found none.
彼女は「危険」と書かれた表示を探したのですが、見つかりませんでした。

7. By now, Alice felt like none of these events were strange at all.
この頃になると、アリスはこれらの出来事のどれもが全く不思議ではないと感じていました。

8. Her tears were falling to the floor and making a pool all around her when she saw the White Rabbit again!
彼女が再び白うさぎを見たときには、彼女の涙は床に落ちて彼女の周りにプールができていました。

9. She is so different from me, for I know many things and Mabel—well, she knows very little.
彼女は私とはとても違っているわ。私はたくさんのことを知っているんだけど、そうね、メイベルはほとんど何も知らないわ。

10. I will see if I still know all the things I used to.
私が以前知っていたことをまだすべて知っているかどうか、確かめてみるわ。

11. As she said this, she looked at herself and saw that she was growing small again.
彼女はそう言いながら自分を見ると、自分がまた小さくなっていることがわかりました。

12. But now she was so small that she was swimming in her own pool of giant tears!
でも、今では彼女はとても小さくなっていて、自分の大粒の涙のプールで泳いでいました。

13. At this, the Mouse jumped in fear and tried to swim away as fast as he could.
これで、ネズミは怖くなって飛び上がり、全力で泳いで逃げようとしました。

14. That was the first thing I learned how to say in French!
それは、私がフランス語で最初に覚えた言い方だったの。

15. So the Mouse began the story and they all listened, but they were not getting any drier.
それで、ネズミは物語を始め、みんなはそれを聞いていましたが、一向に彼らが乾くことはありませんでした。

16. All the racers stood here and there along a race course that was a strange shape.
すべての選手たちは、奇妙な形をしたレースコースのあちこちに立ちました。

17. "You said you would tell me about why you don't like cats," said Alice.
「猫が嫌いな理由を話してくれるって言ってたわよね」とアリスが言いました。

18. "I wish Dinah were here," said Alice.
「ダイナがここにいてくれたらいいのに」とアリスは言いました。

19. Alice ran in the direction the White Rabbit was pointing to.
アリスは白うさぎが指差した方向に走りました。

20. She was just about to take them back to the Rabbit when she saw a little bottle.
彼女はそれらをうさぎに持ち帰ろうとしたところで、小さなびんを見つけました。

21. She put her foot out the door and her arm through the window.
彼女は足をドアから、腕を窓から出しました。

22. The animals started to chase her but she ran until she was safe in a forest.
動物たちは彼女を追いかけ始めましたが、彼女は森の中で安全になるまで走り続けました。

23. Alice walked through the forest not knowing what to do.
アリスは何をすべきかわからないまま、森の中を歩きました。

24. I knew who I was yesterday, but today I don't know.
昨日までは自分が誰かわかっていたのに、今日はわからないんです。

25. She ate a little of each piece until she was finally her usual size.
彼女は最終的にいつものサイズになるまで、それぞれを少しずつ食べました。

26. He was opening a letter that was being delivered by a fish.
彼は、魚によって届けられた手紙を開いていました。

27. The frog didn't answer any of Alice's questions in a sensible way.
カエルはアリスの質問に何一つ理にかなった答えをしませんでした。

28. Alice ran out of the house with the baby to keep it safe.
アリスは赤ちゃんを守るために、赤ちゃんを連れて家を飛び出しました。

29. Now she did not know what to do so she walked through the forest until she came to a cat sitting in a tree.
どうすればいいのかわからないので、彼女は森の中を歩いていると、木の上に猫が座っているのが見えてきました。

30. Alice thanked the Cheshire Cat for the directions.
アリスは道案内をしてくれたチェシャ猫にお礼を言いました。

31. The table was set with many cups for a tea party.
テーブルにはお茶会用のカップがたくさん置かれていました。

32. "Putting butter in my broken watch did not fix it," said the Hatter to the Hare.
「バターを私の壊れた時計に入れても直らないんだ」と帽子屋はうさぎに言いました。

33. They all got up and moved over one seat to where there was a new tea cup.
全員が立ち上がり、新しいティーカップのある席に移動しました。

34. She ate some mushroom until she was the right size to pick up the little golden key on the table.
彼女は、テーブルの上の小さな金色のカギを拾うのにちょうどいい大きさになるまで、キノコを食べました。

35. In the rose garden, three playing cards were painting a tree of white roses red.
バラ園では、3枚のトランプのカードが白いバラの木を赤く塗っていました。

36. She knew they were just playing cards and she was not afraid of them.
彼女は彼らがただのトランプのカードだと知っていたので、怖くはありませんでした。

37. The Queen saw the three playing cards and a white rose that was half painted.
女王は3枚のカードと、半分だけ塗られた白いバラを見ました。

38. "The Queen has ordered her head to be cut off," said the White Rabbit.

「女王は彼女の首を切るように命じたんだ」と白うさぎが言いました。

39. Alice thought it was the strangest croquet ground she had ever seen.
アリスは今まで見た中で一番奇妙なクロッケー場だと思いました。

40. But when she got the flamingo in position, it always moved and looked up into her face.
しかし、彼女がフラミンゴを位置につかせると、フラミンゴはいつも動いて彼女の顔を見上げてのぞき込みました。

41. She had not had any problems with the Queen, but it could happen any time.
彼女は女王との間には何の問題もありませんでしたが、いつそれが起こるかわかりません。

42. She hurried to find her flamingo, but when she came back, the hedgehog was gone again.
彼女は急いでフラミンゴを探しに行きましたが、戻ってきたときにはハリネズミはまたいなくなっていました。

43. "But it doesn't matter much," thought Alice, "because the cards who are making the arches have left as well."
「でも、アーチを作っているカードたちも帰ってしまったから、あまり意味がないわ」とアリスは思いました。

44. But the Cat disappeared by the time he came back with the Duchess.
しかし、彼が公爵夫人と一緒に戻ってきた時には猫は消えていました。

45. She thought to herself that maybe it was only the pepper that had made the Duchess so angry when they met in the kitchen.
アリスは、台所で会った時に公爵夫人をとても怒らせたのは、もしかしたら胡椒のせいかもしれないと思いました。

46. Alice did not like it, but she wanted to be polite so she did not protest.
アリスはそれが気に入りませんでしたが、礼儀正しくしたかったので抗議はしませんでした。

47. Then she left to make sure the Executioner was doing his job.
そして、彼女は処刑人が仕事をしているかどうかを確認するために去っていきました。

48. Alice was worried, but the Gryphon laughed and told Alice that no one actually had their heads cut off.

アリスは心配しましたが、グリフォンは笑って、実際に首を切られた人はいないとアリスに言いました。

49. At last the Mock Turtle said, "When we were little, we went to school by the sea, where we were taught by an old turtle called 'Tortoise.'"
最後に、にせウミガメはこう言いました。「私たちが小さかった頃、私たちは海辺の学校に通っていて、『トータス』と呼ばれる年老いたカメに教えてもらっていました」

50. "We went to school every day and studied French, music, and washing—as well as the usual subjects like mathematics, reading, writing, and uglification."
「私たちは毎日学校に通い、フランス語、音楽、洗濯などのほか、数学、読み書き、醜化などの通常の科目を勉強しました」

51. "Perhaps you have never met a lobster, so you have no idea what a wonderful dance a Lobster-Quadrille is!"
「おそらく君はロブスターに会ったことがないだろうから、ロブスター・カドリールがどんな素晴らしいダンスなのかわからないだろうね」

52. They went on to explain the steps of the dance in detail.
彼らは続いて、そのダンスのステップを詳しく説明してくれました。

53. The Mock Turtle asked if Alice had ever seen a whiting.
にせウミガメはアリスに、ホワイティングを見たことがあるかと尋ねました。

54. The Mock Turtle closed his eyes, so the Gryphon explained that they got their tails stuck in their mouths while dancing with the lobsters at sea.
にせウミガメが目を閉じたので、グリフォンは「海でロブスターと踊っていると、尾が口に詰まってしまうんだよ」と説明しました。

55. As she talked, her listeners began standing very close to her, very quietly, with their mouths wide open.
彼女が話している間、彼女の聴衆は彼女の非常に近くに、非常に静かに、口を大きく開いて立っていました。

56. The Mock Turtle began singing 'Turtle Soup,' although he had to take breaks to cry.
にせウミガメは「ウミガメのスープ」を歌い始めましたが、泣くために中断しなければなりませんでした。

57. The White Rabbit said that the Knave of Hearts was accused of taking the Queen's tarts.
白うさぎは、ハートのジャックが女王のタルトを取ったと告発されていると言いました。

58. "If you don't, I will have you killed."
「もしあなたがそうしなければ、私はあなたを殺してもらいます」

59. Alice was beginning to grow larger again, but she decided to stay where she was as long as there was room.
アリスは再び大きくなり始めていましたが、余裕がある限り自分の居場所に留まることにしました。

60. Imagine her surprise when the White Rabbit read out the name, "Alice!"
白うさぎが「アリス！」と名前を読み上げた時の彼女の驚きを想像してみてください。

61. She bumped into the jury box, knocking all of the animals over.
アリスは陪審員席にぶつかり、動物たちをすべて倒してしまいました。

62. When the jurors were sitting again, the King asked Alice, "What do you know about this business?"
陪審員が再び座っていたとき、王はアリスに「この事件について何を知っていますか?」と尋ねました。

63. The Queen was ready to have the Knave's head cut off.
女王はジャックの頭を切り落とす準備ができていました。

64. "Let the jury tell us what they think," the King said.
「陪審員の意見を聞こう」と王様は言いました。

65. "The jurors can tell us what they think after we have decided what to do with the Knave."
「陪審員がどう思うかを言うのは、我々がジャックをどうするか決めた後でいい」

66. But she suddenly found herself lying by the river with her head on her sister's leg.
しかし、彼女はふと気づくと、川辺に横たわり、姉の脚に頭を乗せていました。

67. Finally, she imagined Alice all grown up and how she would keep her simple, child's heart.
最後に、アリスが大人になり、そして彼女がどのようにして、素朴な子どもの心を保つだろうか想像しました。

68. Maybe she would tell her own children about her happy summer days as a child, and about her dream of Wonderland long ago.
彼女は自分の子どもたちに、子どもの頃の楽しい夏の日々や、昔見た不思議の国の夢を語るのかもしれません。

Word List

A B C D E F G H I J K L M N O P Q R S T U V W X Y Z

・語形が規則変化する語の見出しは原形で示しています。不規則変化語は本文中で使われている形になっています。

・一般的な意味を紹介していますので、一部の語で本文で実際に使われている品詞や意味と合っていないことがあります。

・品詞は以下のように示しています。

[名]名詞	[代]代名詞	[形]形容詞	[副]副詞	[動]動詞	[助]助動詞
[前]前置詞	[接]接続詞	[間]間投詞	[冠]冠詞	[略]略語	[俗]俗語
[熟]熟語	[頭]接頭語	[尾]接尾語	[記]記号	[関]関係代名詞	

A

□ **a** [冠] ①1つの，1人の，ある ②～につき

□ **about** [副] ①およそ，約 ②まわりに，あたりを **be about to** まさに～しようとしている，～するところだ [前] ①～について ②～のまわりに[の] **care about** ～を気に掛ける

□ **accuse** [動]《－of ～》～(の理由)で告訴[非難]する **accused of**《be －》～で告発される

□ **act** [動] ①行動する ②演じる **act as** ～の役を務める

□ **actually** [副] 実際に，本当に，実は

□ **adventure** [名] 冒険

□ **afraid** [形] ①心配して ②恐れて，こわがって **afraid of** ～を恐れる

□ **after** [前] ①～の後に[で]，～の次に ②《前後に名詞がきて》次々に～，何度も～《反復・継続を表す》 **after a while** しばらくして(から) **run after** ～を追いかける [接] (～した)後に[で]

□ **again** [副] 再び，もう一度

□ **against** [前] ①～に対して，～に反対して，(規則など)に違反して ②～にもたれて **push against** ～を押す

□ **ago** [副] ～前に **long ago** ずっと以前に

□ **agree** [動] ①同意する ②意見が一致する

□ **air** [名]《the －》空中，空間

□ **Alice** [名] アリス《人名》

□ **alive** [形] 生きている

□ **all** [形] すべての，～中 **all kinds of** さまざまな，あらゆる種類の [名] 全体 **all in all** 全体から見て **at all** 全く～ない《否定文で》 **not ~ at all** 少しも[全然] ～ない **with all** ～がありながら [副] まったく，すっかり

□ **alone** [形] ただひとりの [副] ひとりで，～だけで

□ **along** 前 ～に沿って 副 ～に沿って，前へ，進んで **along with** ～と一緒に

□ **also** 副 ～も(また)，～も同様に 接 その上，さらに

□ **although** 接 ～だけれども，～にもかかわらず，たとえ～でも

□ **always** 副 いつも，常に

□ **am** 動 ～である，(～に)いる[ある]《主語がIのときのbeの現在形》

□ **an** 冠 ①1つの，1人の，ある ②～につき

□ **and** 接 ①そして，～と… ②《同じ語を結んで》ますます ③《結果を表して》それで，だから

□ **angrily** 副 怒って，腹立たしげに

□ **angry** 形 怒って，腹を立てて

□ **animal** 名 動物

□ **another** 形 ①もう1つ[1人]の ②別の

□ **answer** 動 答える，応じる

□ **ant** 名 アリ

□ **any** 形 ①《疑問文で》何か，いくつかの ②《否定文で》何も，少しも(～ない) ③《肯定文で》どの～も **any time** いつでも **not ~ any** 一つも～ない 代 ①《疑問文で》(～のうち)何か，どれか，誰か ②《否定文で》少しも，何も[誰も]～ない ③《肯定文で》どれも，誰でも

□ **anybody** 代 ①《疑問文・条件節で》誰か ②《否定文で》誰も(～ない) ③《肯定文で》誰でも

□ **anymore** 副 《通例否定文，疑問文で》今はもう，これ以上，これから

□ **appear** 動 ①現れる，見えてくる ②(～のように)見える，～らしい

□ **arch** 名 アーチ，(アーチ状の)門[道]

□ **are** 動 ～である，(～に)いる[ある]《主語がyou, we, theyまたは複数名詞のときのbeの現在形》

□ **arm** 名 腕

□ **around** 前 ～のまわりに，～のあちこちに 副 ①まわりに，あちこちに ②およそ，約 **go around** 動き回る，あちらこちらに行く **turn around** 振り向く，向きを変える，方向転換する

□ **arrive** 動 到着する，到達する **arrive at** ～に着く

□ **as** 接 ①《as ~ as …の形で》…と同じくらい～ ②～のとおりに，～のように ③～しながら，～しているときに ④～するにつれて，～にしたがって ⑤～なので ⑥～だけれども ⑦～する限りでは 前 ①～として(の) ②～の時 副 同じくらい **act as** ～の役を務める **as long as** ～する以上は，～である限りは **as much as** ～と同じだけ **as soon as** ～するとすぐ，～するや否や **as well** 同様に **as well as** ～と同様に **as ~ as one can** できる限り～

□ **ask** 動 ①尋ねる，聞く ②頼む，求める **ask if** ～かどうかを尋ねる

□ **asleep** 形 眠って(いる状態の) 副 眠って，休止して

□ **at** 前 ①《場所・時》～に[で] ②《目標・方向》～に[を]，～に向かって ③《原因・理由》～を見て[聞いて・知って] ④～に従事して，～の状態で **at all** 全く～ない《否定文で》 at last やっと，ようやく **at the time** そのころ，当時は **at this** これを見て，そこで（すぐに） **not ～ at all** 少しも［全然］～ない

□ **ate** 動 eat（食べる）の過去

□ **away** 副 離れて，遠くに，去って，わきに **get away** 逃げる，逃亡する **move away** 立ち去る **run away** 走り去る，逃げ出す **walk away** 立ち去る，遠ざかる

B

□ **baby** 名 ①赤ん坊 ②《呼びかけで》あなた

□ **back** 副 ①戻って ②後ろへ［に］ **come back** 戻る **get ～ back** ～を取り返す［戻す］ **go back to** ～に帰る［戻る］，～に遡る，（中断していた作業に）再び取り掛かる 形 裏の，後ろの

□ **bad** 形 悪い，へたな，まずい

□ **ball** 名 ボール，球

□ **be** 動 ～である，（～に）いる［ある］，～となる **seem to be** ～であるように思われる **want to be** ～の状態でありたいと思う 助 ①《現在分詞とともに用いて》～している ②《過去分詞とともに用いて》～される，～されている

□ **beach** 名 海辺，浜

□ **beautiful** 形 美しい，すばらしい

□ **beautify** 動 美しくする

□ **because** 接（なぜなら）～だから，～という理由［原因］で

□ **become** 動 ①（～に）なる ②（～に）似合う ③becomeの過去分詞

□ **before** 副 以前に

□ **began** 動 begin（始まる）の過去

□ **begin** 動 始まる［始める］，起こる

□ **behind** 前 ～の後ろに，～の背後に

□ **belong** 動《－to ～》～に属する，～のものである

□ **best** 形 最もよい，最大［多］の

□ **better** 形 ①よりよい ②（人が）回復して

□ **big** 形 ①大きい ②偉い，重要な

□ **bird** 名 鳥

□ **bite** 名 かむこと，ひと口 **take a bite** 一口かじる

□ **body** 名 体，胴体

□ **book** 名 本，書物

□ **bottle** 名 瓶，ボトル

□ **box** 名 ①箱，容器 ②観覧席 ③詰所 **jury box** 陪審員席

□ **bread** 名 パン

□ **break** 名 小休止 **take a break** 中断する

□ **bring** 動 ①持ってくる，連れてくる ②もたらす，生じる

□ **broken** 形 破れた，壊れた

□ **bump** 動 ①ドスン［バン］と当たる ②ぶつかる，ぶつける **bump into**（～に）衝突する，ぶつかる

□ **bunch** 名 房，束，群れ **a bunch of** 1束の

□ **business** 名〔困難で厄介な〕状況，問題

□ **but** 接 ①でも，しかし ②～を除いて **not ～ but …** ～ではなくて… **nothing but**《be －》～にすぎない

□ **butter** 名バター

□ **by** 前 ①《位置》～のそばに[で] ②《手段・方法・行為者・基準》～によって，～で ③《期限》～までには ④《通過・経由》～を経由して，～を通って **by now** 今頃はもう **by the time** ～する時までに 副そばに，通り過ぎて **run by** 走り過ぎる

C

□ **cake** 名菓子，ケーキ

□ **call** 動呼ぶ，叫ぶ **call out** 叫ぶ，掛け声をかける

□ **came** 動come（来る）の過去

□ **can** 助 ①～できる ②～してもよい ③～でありうる ④《否定文で》～のはずがない **Can you ～?** ～してくれますか。 **as ～ as one can** できる限り～

□ **capital** 名首都

□ **card** 名 ①カード，券，名刺，はがき ②トランプ **playing card** トランプのカード

□ **care** 動 ①《通例否定文・疑問文で》気にする，心配する ②世話をする **care about** ～を気に掛ける

□ **careful** 形注意深い，慎重な

□ **carry** 動運ぶ，連れていく，持ち歩く

□ **cat** 名ネコ（猫）

□ **catch** 動つかまえる

□ **caterpillar** 名いも虫，毛虫

□ **caucus** 名幹部会議，党員集会

□ **ceiling** 名天井

□ **chair** 名いす

□ **change** 動変わる，変える **change places** 席を替わる

□ **chase** 動 ①追跡する，追い[探し]求める ②追い立てる

□ **cheer** 動かっさいを送る

□ **Cheshire Cat** チェシャ猫

□ **child** 名子ども

□ **children** 名child（子ども）の複数

□ **close** 形 ①近い ②親しい ③狭い 動 ①閉まる，閉める ②終える，閉店する

□ **closed** 動close（閉まる）の過去，過去分詞 形閉じた，閉鎖した

□ **cloud** 名雲，雲状のもの，煙

□ **come** 動 ①来る，行く，現れる ②（出来事が）起こる，生じる ③～になる ④comeの過去分詞 **come back** 戻る **come in** 中にはいる，やってくる **come on** さあ来なさい **come through** 通り抜ける，通り過ぎる **come up to** ～のすぐそばまでやってくる

□ **confused** 形困惑した，混乱した **get confused** 当惑する

□ **confusing** 形混乱させる，紛らわしい

□ **continue** 動続く，続ける，（中断後）再開する，（ある方向に）移動していく

□ **cook** 名料理人，コック

□ **corner** 名曲がり角，角

□ **could** 助 ①can（～できる）の過去 ②《控え目な推量・可能性・願望などを表す》 **Could you ～?** ～し

てくださいますか。

☐ **course** 名 ①進路, 方向 ②経過, 成り行き ③科目, 講座 ④策, 方策 **of course** もちろん, 当然

☐ **court** 名 ①廷臣, 臣下 ②法廷, 裁判所

☐ **crazy** 形 狂気の, ばかげた, 無茶な

☐ **croquet** 名《競技》クロッケー

☐ **cry** 動 泣く, 叫ぶ, 大声を出す, 嘆く 名 泣き声, 叫び, かっさい

☐ **cup** 名 ①カップ, 茶わん ②賞杯, 競技大会

☐ **curtain** 名 カーテン

☐ **cut** 動 ①切る, 刈る ②短縮する, 削る ③cutの過去, 過去分詞 **cut off** 切断する, 切り離す **cut off someone's head** (人)の首をはねる

D

☐ **dance** 動 踊る, ダンスをする 名 ダンス, ダンスパーティー

☐ **dangerous** 形 危険な, 有害な

☐ **dark** 形 ①暗い, 闇の ②(色が)濃い, (髪が)黒い ③陰うつな

☐ **day** 名 ①日中, 昼間 ②日, 期日 ③《-s》時代, 生涯 **every day** 毎日

☐ **dear** 形 いとしい, 親愛なる, 大事な 間 まあ, おや **Oh, dear!** あらまあ。

☐ **decide** 動 決定[決意]する, (〜しようと)決める, 判決を下す

☐ **declare** 動 ①宣言する ②断言する

☐ **deep** 形 ①深い, 深さ〜の ②深遠な

☐ **deliver** 動 ①配達する, 伝える ②達成する, 果たす

☐ **demand** 動 ①要求する, 尋ねる ②必要とする

☐ **detail** 名 細部, 《-s》詳細 **in detail** 詳細に

☐ **did** 動 do (〜をする) の過去 助 doの過去

☐ **different** 形 異なった, 違った, 別の, さまざまな **be different from** 〜と違う

☐ **difficult** 形 困難な, むずかしい, 扱いにくい

☐ **Dinah** 名 ダイナ《猫の名》

☐ **direction** 名 方向, 方角

☐ **disagree** 動 異議を唱える, 反対する

☐ **disappear** 動 見えなくなる, 姿を消す, なくなる

☐ **discuss** 動 議論[検討]する

☐ **distance** 名 距離, 隔たり, 遠方 **in the distance** 遠方に

☐ **do** 助 ①《ほかの動詞とともに用いて現在形の否定文・疑問文をつくる》 ②《同じ動詞を繰り返す代わりに用いる》 ③《動詞を強調するのに用いる》 動 〜をする

☐ **dodo** 名 ①ドードー《17世紀末に絶滅した飛べない大型の鳥》 ②のろま, あほ, 時代遅れの人

☐ **does** 助 doの3人称単数現在

☐ **door** 名 ドア, 戸 **fit through the door** ドアを通り抜ける

☐ **down** 前 〜の下方へ, 〜を下って

副 ①下へ, 降りて, 低くなって ②倒れて fall straight down まっすぐに落ちる get down 身をかがめる jump down 飛び降りる look down at ～に目[視線]を落とす put down 下に置く, 下ろす run down 駆け下りる

□ **dream** 名 夢, 幻想 動 (～の)夢を見る, 夢想[想像]する

□ **drink** 動 飲む safe to drink 飲んでも安全である

□ **drop** 動 (ぽたぽた)落ちる, 落とす

□ **dry** 形 乾燥した get dry 乾く

□ **Duchess** 名 公爵夫人

□ **duck** 名 カモ, アヒル

E

□ **each** 形 それぞれの, 各自の each other お互いに

□ **eaglet** 名 ワシの子

□ **eat** 動 食べる, 食事する

□ **else** 副 ①そのほかに[の], 代わりに ②さもないと somebody else 誰か他の人

□ **end** 動 終わる, 終える

□ **English** 名 英語

□ **enough** 形 十分な, (～するに)足る enough to ～するのに十分な 副 (～できる)だけ, 十分に, まったく

□ **event** 名 出来事, 事件, イベント

□ **ever** 副 今までに, これまで, かつて, いつまでも

□ **every** 形 ①どの～も, すべての, あらゆる ②毎～, ～ごとの every day 毎日 every second 刻々と

□ **everybody** 代 誰でも, 皆

□ **everyone** 代 誰でも, 皆

□ **everything** 代 すべてのこと[もの], 何でも, 何もかも

□ **evidence** 名 ①証拠, 証人 ②形跡

□ **excited** 形 興奮した, わくわくした

□ **excuse** 動 ①(～の)言い訳をする ②許す, 容赦する, 免除する

□ **executioner** 名 死刑執行人

□ **explain** 動 説明する, 明らかにする, 釈明[弁明]する

□ **eye** 名 目

F

□ **face** 名 顔

□ **fall** 動 落ちる, 倒れる fall straight down まっすぐに落ちる

□ **fan** 名 扇(状のもの), うちわ 動 あおぐ, あおる

□ **fast** 副 速く, 急いで

□ **fear** 名 ①恐れ ②心配, 不安 in fear おびえて with fear 怖がって

□ **feel** 動 感じる, (～と)思う feel like ～のような感じがする

□ **feet** 名 ①foot(足)の複数 ②フィート《長さの単位。約30cm》

□ **fell** 動 fall(落ちる)の過去

□ **felt** 動 feel(感じる)の過去, 過去分詞

□ **few** 形 ①ほとんどない, 少数の(～しかない) ②《a－》少数の, 少しは

ある

□ **fight** 動(～と)戦う, 争う **fight with** ～と戦う

□ **fill** 動 ①満ちる, 満たす ②《be -ed with ～》～でいっぱいである **fill up** (穴・すき間を)いっぱいに満たす, 詰める **fill up with** ～でいっぱいになる

□ **finally** 副最後に, ついに, 結局

□ **find** 動 ①見つける ②(～と)わかる, 気づく, ～と考える ③得る

□ **fine** 形 ①元気な ②美しい, りっぱな, 申し分ない, 結構な ③晴れた

□ **finish** 動終わる, 終える

□ **first** 形 ①第一の, 最初の ②最も重要な 副第一に, 最初に

□ **fish** 名魚

□ **fit** 動合致[適合]する, 合致させる **fit through the door** ドアを通り抜ける

□ **five** 名5(の数字), 5人[個] 形5の, 5人[個]の

□ **fix** 動修理する

□ **flamingo** 名フラミンゴ

□ **floor** 名床, 階

□ **flower** 名花, 草花

□ **follow** 動ついていく, あとをたどる

□ **foot** 名足

□ **for** 前 ①《目的・原因・対象》～にとって, ～のために[の], ～に対して ②《期間》～間 ③《代理》～の代わりに ④《方向》～へ(向かって) 接というわけは～, なぜなら～, だから

□ **forest** 名森林

□ **forgot** 動forget(忘れる)の過去, 過去分詞

□ **forty** 名40(の数字), 40人[個] 形40の, 40人[個]の

□ **forward** 副 ①前方に ②先へ, 進んで

□ **found** 動 ①find(見つける)の過去, 過去分詞 ②～の基礎を築く, ～を設立する

□ **four** 名4(の数字), 4人[個] 形4の, 4人[個]の

□ **French** 名フランス語

□ **friend** 名友だち, 仲間

□ **friendly** 形親しみのある, 親切な, 友情のこもった

□ **frog** 名カエル(蛙)

□ **from** 前 ①《出身・出発点・時間・順序・原料》～から ②《原因・理由》～がもとで

□ **front** 名正面, 前 **in front of** ～の前に, ～の正面に

□ **full** 形 ①満ちた, いっぱいの, 満期の ②完全な, 盛りの, 充実した

G

□ **game** 名ゲーム, 試合, 遊び, 競技

□ **garden** 名庭, 庭園

□ **gave** 動give(与える)の過去

□ **generally** 副 ①一般に, だいたい ②たいてい

□ **get** 動 ①得る, 手に入れる ②(ある状態に)なる, いたる ③わかる, 理解する ④～させる, ～を(…の状態に)する ⑤(ある場所に)達する,

着く **get away** 逃げる, 逃亡する **get confused** 当惑する **get down** 身をかがめる **get dry** 乾く **get out of** ～から外へ出る **get sleepy** 眠くなる **get smaller** 小さくなる **get through** ～を通り抜ける **get tired** 疲れる, 飽きが来る **get to** ～に達する **get up** 立ち上がる **get ~ back** ～を取り返す[戻す] **get ~ in position** ～を定位置につける **How are you getting on?** どうしてる?《あいさつ》

□ **giant** 名巨人 形巨大な

□ **girl** 名女の子, 少女

□ **glad** 形 ①うれしい, 喜ばしい ②《be – to ~》～してうれしい, 喜んで～する

□ **glove** 名手袋, グローブ

□ **go** 動 ①行く, 出かける ②動く ③進む, 経過する, いたる ④(ある状態に)なる **be going to** ～するつもりである **go around** 動き回る, あちらこちらに行く **go back to** ～に帰る[戻る], ～に遡る, (中断していた作業に)再び取り掛かる **go into** ～に入る **go off** 立ち去る **go on** 起こる, 発生する **go on to** 次に～する **go through** 通り抜ける

□ **golden** 形 ①金色の ②金製の

□ **gone** 形去った

□ **good** 形よい, 上手な, 優れた 間よかった, わかった, よろしい

□ **got** 動 get (得る) の過去, 過去分詞

□ **grew** 動 grow (成長する) の過去

□ **grin** 動歯を見せて笑う

□ **ground** 名地面, 土, 土地 **on the ground** 地面に

□ **group** 名集団, 群

□ **grow** 動 ①成長する, 育つ, 育てる ②増大する, 大きくなる, (次第に～に)なる **grow up** 成長する, 大人になる

□ **grown** 形成長した, 成人した **grown up** 成長した

□ **Gryphon** 名グリフォン《想像上の動物》

H

□ **had** 動 have (持つ) の過去, 過去分詞 助 haveの過去《過去完了の文をつくる》 **I wish I hadn't done** ～しなければよかったのに(してしまった)

□ **half** 副半分, なかば, 不十分に

□ **hallway** 名玄関, 廊下

□ **hand** 名手

□ **handwriting** 名 ①手書き, 肉筆 ②筆跡, 書体

□ **happen** 動 ①(出来事が)起こる, 生じる ②偶然[たまたま] ～する

□ **happily** 副幸福に, 楽しく, うまく, 幸いにも

□ **happy** 形幸せな, うれしい, 幸運な, 満足して **be happy to** ～してうれしい, 喜んで～する

□ **hard** 形堅い

□ **Hare** 名野うさぎ

□ **has** 助 haveの3人称単数現在《現在完了の文をつくる》

□ **Hatter** 名帽子屋

□ **have** 動 ①持つ, 持っている, 抱

く ②(〜が)ある, いる ③食べる, 飲む ④経験する, (病気に)かかる ⑤催す, 開く ⑥(人に) 〜させる **have to** 〜しなければならない **have no idea** わからない **have someone killed** (人)を殺させる 助《〈have＋過去分詞〉の形で現在完了の文をつくる》〜した, 〜したことがある, ずっと〜している **should have done** 〜すべきだった(のにしなかった)《仮定法》**will have done** 〜してしまっているだろう《未来完了形》

□ **he** 代 彼は[が]

□ **head** 名 ①頭 ②先頭 ③長, 指導者 **cut off someone's head** (人)の首をはねる **Off with someone's head!** 〜の首をはねろ。

□ **hear** 動 聞く, 聞こえる **hear of** 〜について聞く

□ **heard** 動 hear (聞く)の過去, 過去分詞

□ **heart** 名 ①心臓, 胸 ②心, 感情, ハート

□ **hedgehog** 名 ハリネズミ, ヤマアラシ

□ **hello** 間 こんにちは, やあ

□ **help** 動 助ける, 手伝う 名 助け, 手伝い

□ **her** 代 ①彼女を[に] ②彼女の

□ **here** 副 ①ここに[で] ②《- is [are] 〜》ここに〜がある ③さあ, そら **here and there** あちこちで

□ **herself** 代 彼女自身

□ **high** 形 高い **a mile high** 1マイルの高さ

□ **him** 代 彼を[に]

□ **his** 代 ①彼の ②彼のもの

□ **history** 名 歴史, 経歴

□ **hit** 動 ①打つ, なぐる ②ぶつける, ぶつかる ③命中する ④hitの過去, 過去分詞

□ **hold** 動 つかむ, 持つ, 抱く

□ **hole** 名 穴, すき間

□ **home** 名 家

□ **hot** 形 暑い, 熱い

□ **house** 名 家 **run out of a house** 家から外に走り出る

□ **how** 副 ①どうやって, どれくらい, どんなふうに ②なんて(〜だろう) ③《関係副詞》〜する方法 **How are you getting on?** どうしてる？《あいさつ》**how to** 〜する方法

□ **hunter** 名 狩りをする人, 狩人, ハンター

□ **hurry** 動 急ぐ, 急がせる **hurry off** 急いで立ち去る

□ **hurt** 動 傷つける, 痛む

I

□ **I** 代 私は[が] **I wish I hadn't done** 〜しなければよかったのに(してしまった)

□ **idea** 名 考え, 意見, アイデア, 計画 **have no idea** わからない

□ **if** 接 もし〜ならば, たとえ〜でも, 〜かどうか **ask if** 〜かどうかを尋ねる **if you please** よろしければ **see if** 〜かどうかを確かめる **wonder if** 〜ではないかと思う

□ **imagine** 動 想像する, 心に思い描く

□ **important** 形重要な, 大切な, 有力な

□ **in** 前①《場所・位置・所属》～(の中)に[で・の] ②《時》～(の時)に[の・で], ～後(に), ～の間(に) ③《方法・手段》～で ④～を身につけて, ～を着て ⑤～に関して, ～について ⑥《状態》～の状態で 副中へ[に], 内へ[に] **in a sensible way** 良識ある態度で **in detail** 詳細に **in fear** おびえて **in front of** ～の前に, ～の正面に **in the distance** 遠方に **in trouble** 困難な状態で

□ **inch** 名インチ《長さの単位。1/12フィート, 2.54cm》 **three inches tall** 身長3インチ

□ **indeed** 副①実際, 本当に ②《強意》まったく

□ **inside** 名内部, 内側 副内部[内側]に

□ **instead** 副その代わりに

□ **interested** 形興味を持った, 関心のある

□ **interesting** 形おもしろい, 興味を起こさせる

□ **interrupt** 動さえぎる, 妨害する, 口をはさむ

□ **into** 前①《動作・運動の方向》～の中へ[に] ②《変化》～に[へ] **bump into** (～に)衝突する, ぶつかる **go into** ～に入る **put ～ into …** ～を…に突っ込む **turn into** ～に変わる[変化する]

□ **invite** 動①招待する, 招く ②勧める, 誘う

□ **is** 動be(～である)の3人称単数現在

□ **it** 代①それは[が], それを[に] ②《天候・日時・距離・寒暖などを示す》

□ **its** 代それの, あれの

J

□ **job** 名仕事, 職

□ **judge** 動判決を下す, 裁く, 判断する, 評価する 名裁判官, 判事

□ **jump** 動①跳ぶ, 跳躍する, 飛び越える, 飛びかかる ②(～を)熱心にやり始める **jump down** 飛び降りる **jump up** 急に立ち上がる

□ **juror** 名陪審員

□ **jury** 名陪審, 陪審員団 **jury box** 陪審員席

□ **just** 副①まさに, ちょうど, (～した)ばかり ②ほんの, 単に, ただ～だけ ③ちょっと **just then** ちょうどその時

K

□ **keep** 動①とっておく, 保つ, 続ける ②(～を…に)しておく ③飼う, 養う ④経営する ⑤守る **keep ～ safe** ～を保護する

□ **kept** 動keep(とっておく)の過去, 過去分詞

□ **key** 名カギ

□ **kill** 動殺す **have someone killed** (人)を殺させる

□ **kind** 名種類 **all kinds of** さまざまな, あらゆる種類の

□ **king** 名王, 国王

□ **kiss** 動キスする

□ **kitchen** 名台所, 調理場

□ **knave** 名〔トランプの〕ジャック

□ **knew** 動know（知っている）の過去

□ **knock** 動ノックする, たたく, ぶつける **knock over** 張り倒す

□ **know** 動知っている, 知る, (～が)わかる, 理解している

L

□ **lady** 名婦人, 夫人, 淑女, 奥さん

□ **land** 動上陸する, 着地する

□ **large** 形①大きい, 広い ②大勢の, 多量の 副大きく

□ **last** 名《the –》最後(のもの), 終わり **at last** やっと, ようやく

□ **late** 形遅い

□ **laugh** 動笑う **make someone laugh**（人）を笑わせる

□ **leaf** 名葉

□ **learn** 動学ぶ, 習う, 教わる, 知識[経験]を得る

□ **leave** 動①出発する, 去る ②残す, 置き忘れる ③(～を…の)ままにしておく ④ゆだねる

□ **leaves** 名leaf（葉）の複数

□ **left** 動leave（去る, ～をあとに残す）の過去, 過去分詞

□ **leg** 名脚, すね

□ **lesson** 名授業, 学科, 課

□ **let** 動（人に～）させる, (～するのを）許す, (～をある状態に）する **let us** どうか私たちに～させてください

□ **letter** 名①手紙 ②文字

□ **lie** 動①横たわる, 寝る ②(ある状態に）ある, 存在する

□ **like** 動好む, 好きである **Would you like ～?** ～はいかがですか **would like to** ～したいと思う 前～に似ている, ～のような 接あたかも～のように。 **feel like** ～のような感じがする **sound like** ～のように聞こえる

□ **line** 名①線, 糸 ②(字の)行 ③列 動①線を引く ②整列する **lined with** ～がずらりと並ぶ

□ **listen** 動《– to ～》～を聞く, ～に耳を傾ける

□ **listener** 名聞く人

□ **little** 形①小さい, 幼い ②少しの, 短い ③ほとんど～ない,《a –》少しはある

□ **live** 動住む, 暮らす, 生きている

□ **lobster** 名ロブスター

□ **Lobster-Quadrille** 名ロブスター・カドリール《ダンス, 舞曲名》

□ **lock** 動錠を下ろす, 閉じ込める

□ **London** 名ロンドン《英国の首都》

□ **lonely** 形①孤独な, 心さびしい ②ひっそりした, 人里離れた

□ **long** 形①長い, 長期の ②《長さ・距離・時間などを示す語句を伴って》～の長さ[距離・時間]の **as long as** ～する以上は, ～である限りは **long ago** ずっと以前に

□ **look** 動①見る ②(～に)見える, (～の)顔つきをする ③注意する **look down at** ～に目[視線]を落とす **look for** ～を探す **look through** ～をのぞき込む **look to**

～の方を向く **look up** 見上げる

□ **lost** 動 lose (失う) の過去, 過去分詞

□ **loud** 副 大声に［で］ **out loud** 大きな声で

□ **loudly** 副 大声で, 騒がしく

□ **luckily** 副 運よく, 幸いにも

□ **lying** 動 lie (横たわる) の現在分詞

M

□ **Mabel** 名 メイベル《人名》

□ **made** 動 make (作る) の過去, 過去分詞

□ **main** 形 主な, 主要な

□ **make** 動 ①作る, 得る ②行う, (～に) なる ③(～を…に) する, (～を…) させる **make much sense** 非常によくわかる **make sense** 意味をなす **make sense of** ～を解明する **make someone laugh** (人) を笑わせる **make sure** 確かめる, 確認する

□ **mallet** 名 打球槌, マレット

□ **many** 形 多数の, たくさんの

□ **Mary Ann** メアリーアン《人名》

□ **mathematics** 名 数学

□ **matter** 動《主に疑問文・否定文で》重要である **not matter** 問題にならない

□ **may** 助 ①～かもしれない ②～してもよい, ～できる

□ **maybe** 副 たぶん, おそらく

□ **me** 代 私を［に］

□ **mean** 動 ①意味する ②(～のつもりで) 言う, 意図する ③～するつもりである

□ **meanwhile** 副 それまでの間, 一方では

□ **met** 動 meet (会う) の過去, 過去分詞

□ **middle** 名 中間, 最中

□ **might** 助《mayの過去》①～かもしれない ②～してもよい, ～できる

□ **mile** 名 マイル《長さの単位。1,609m **a mile high** 1マイルの高さ

□ **minute** 名 ①(時間の) 分 ②ちょっとの間

□ **mock** 形 うわべの, まがいの, 模擬の

□ **Mock Turtle** にせウミガメ

□ **more** 形 ①もっと多くの ②それ以上の, 余分の 副 もっと, さらに多く, いっそう **more than** ～以上 名 もっと多くの物［人］

□ **mouse** 名 (ハツカ) ネズミ

□ **mouth** 名 ①口 ②言葉, 発言

□ **move** 動 ①動く, 動かす ②感動させる ③引っ越す, 移動する **move away** 立ち去る **move over** 移動する

□ **much** 形 (量・程度が) 多くの, 多量の 副 ①とても, たいへん ②《比較級・最上級を修飾して》ずっと, はるかに **as much as** ～と同じだけ **make much sense** 非常によくわかる **too much** 過度の

□ **mushroom** 名 キノコ

□ **music** 名 音楽, 楽曲

□ **must** 助 ①～しなければならない

②～に違いない

□ **my** 代 私の

N

□ **name** 名 名前

□ **neck** 名 首

□ **need** 動 (～を)必要とする, 必要である

□ **neighbor** 名 隣人, 隣り合うもの

□ **nervous** 形 ①神経の ②神経質な, おどおどした

□ **never** 副 決して[少しも] ～ない, 一度も[二度と] ～ない

□ **new** 形 ①新しい, 新規の ②新鮮な, できたての

□ **next** 形 ①次の, 翌～ ②隣の

□ **nice** 形 すてきな, よい, きれいな, 親切な

□ **nice-looking** 形 ルックス[顔立ち]の良い

□ **night** 名 夜, 晩

□ **nine** 名 9(の数字), 9人[個] 形 9の, 9人[個]の

□ **no** 副 ①いいえ, いや ②少しも～ない **have no idea** わからない 形 ～がない, 少しも～ない, ～どころでない, ～禁止

□ **no one** 代 誰も[一人も] ～ない

□ **nobody** 代 誰も[一人も] ～ない

□ **nod** 動 うなずく

□ **none** 代 (～の)何も[誰も・少しも]…ない

□ **nonsense** 名 ばかげたこと, ナンセンス

□ **normal** 形 普通の, 平均の, 標準的な

□ **not** 副 ～でない, ～しない **not matter** 問題にならない **not ～ any** 一つも～ない **not ～ at all** 少しも[全然] ～ない **not ～ but** … ～ではなくて…

□ **note** 名 メモ, 覚え書き **take notes** 記録を取る

□ **nothing** 代 何も～ない[しない] **nothing but** 《be –》 ～にすぎない

□ **notice** 動 気づく, 認める

□ **now** 副 ①今(では), 現在 ②今すぐに ③では, さて 名 今, 現在 **by now** 今頃はもう

O

□ **of** 前 ①《所有・所属・部分》～の, ～に属する ②《性質・特徴・材料》～の, ～製の ③《部分》～のうち ④《分離・除去》～から

□ **off** 副 ①離れて ②はずれて ③止まって ④休んで **cut off** 切断する, 切り離す **go off** 立ち去る **hurry off** 急いで立ち去る **off with** (すばやく) ～を取り去る **Off with someone's head!** ～の首をはねろ。 **run off** 走り去る, 逃げ去る **set off** 出発する 前 ～を離れて, ～をはずれて, (値段が) ～引きの **cut off someone's head** (人)の首をはねる

□ **oh** 間 ああ, おや, まあ **Oh, dear!** あらまあ。

□ **old** 形 ①年取った, 老いた ②～歳の ③古い, 昔の **old thing** 旧友《英俗》

□ **on** 前 ①《場所・接触》～(の上)に ②《日・時》～に，～と同時に，～のすぐ後で ③《関係・従事》～に関して，～について，～して **on the ground** 地面に **on top of** ～の上(部)に 副 ①身につけて，上に ②前へ，続けて

□ **once** 副 ①一度，1回 ②かつて

□ **one** 名 1(の数字)，1人[個] **no one** 誰も[一人も]～ない **one of** ～の1つ[人] 形 ①1の，1人[個]の ②ある～ ③《the –》唯一の **one side** 片側 代 ①(一般の)人，ある物 ②一方，片方 ③～なもの

□ **only** 副 ①単に，～にすぎない，ただ～だけ ②やっと

□ **open** 形 開いた，広々とした

□ **or** 接 ①～か…，または ②さもないと ③すなわち，言い換えると

□ **order** 動 ①(～するよう)命じる，注文する ②整頓する，整理する

□ **other** 形 ①ほかの，異なった ②(2つのうち)もう一方の，(3つ以上のうち)残りの 代 ①ほかの人[物] ②《the –》残りの1つ **each other** お互いに

□ **our** 代 私たちの

□ **out** 副 ①外へ[に]，不在で，離れて ②世に出て ③消えて ④すっかり 形 ①外の，遠く離れた ②公表された 前 ～から外へ[に] **call out** 叫ぶ，掛け声をかける **get out of** ～から外へ出る **out loud** 大きな声で **out of** ～から外へ，～から抜け出して **point out** ～を指摘する **put out** 外に出す **read out** 読み上げる **run out of a house** 家から外に走り出る **rush out of** 急いで～から出てくる **take out** 取り出す **take out of** ～から出す **take ～ out of one's pocket** ポケットから～を取り出す **try out** 試してみる **way out** 出口 **way out of** ～から抜け出る道

□ **outside** 名 外部，外側 副 外へ，外側に

□ **over** 前 ①～の上の[に]，～を一面に覆って ②～を越えて，～以上に，～よりまさって ③～の向こう側の[に] ④～の間 副 上に，一面に，ずっと **knock over** 張り倒す **move over** 移動する 形 ①上部の，上位の，過多の ②終わって，すんで **be over** 終わる

□ **own** 形 自身の

P

□ **paint** 動 ①ペンキを塗る ②(絵の具などで)描く

□ **pair** 名 (2つから成る)一対，一組，ペア

□ **paper** 名 ①紙 ②書類

□ **Paris** 名 パリ《フランスの首都》

□ **part** 名 部分

□ **party** 名 パーティー，会

□ **people** 名 ①(一般に)人々 ②民衆，国民

□ **pepper** 名 コショウ(胡椒)

□ **perhaps** 副 たぶん，ことによると

□ **person** 名 人

□ **pick** 動 ①(花・果実などを)摘む，もぐ ②選ぶ，精選する **pick up** 拾い上げる，手に入れる

□ **piece** 名一片, 部分

□ **pig** 名ブタ(豚)

□ **place** 名 ①場所, 建物 ②余地, 空間 ③《one's - 》家, 部屋 **change places** 席を替わる

□ **plate** 名(浅い)皿

□ **play** 動遊ぶ, 競技する

□ **player** 名競技者, 選手

□ **playing card** トランプのカード

□ **please** 動喜ばす, 満足させる **if you please** よろしければ 間どうぞ, お願いします

□ **pocket** 名ポケット **take ~ out of one's pocket** ポケットから~を取り出す

□ **poem** 名詩

□ **point** 動 ①(~を)指す, 向ける ②とがらせる **point out** ~を指摘する

□ **polite** 形ていねいな, 礼儀正しい, 洗練された

□ **pool** 名水たまり, プール

□ **porpoise** 名ネズミイルカ

□ **position** 名 ①位置, 場所, 姿勢 ②地位, 身分, 職 ③立場, 状況 **get ~ in position** ~を定位置につける 動置く, 配置する

□ **pretty** 形かわいい, きれいな

□ **prison** 名刑務所, 監獄

□ **prize** 名賞, 賞品, 賞金

□ **problem** 名問題, 難問

□ **protest** 動 ①主張[断言]する ②抗議する, 反対する

□ **push** 動 ①押す, 押し進む, 押し進める ②進む, 突き出る **push against** ~を押す

□ **put** 動 ①置く, のせる ②入れる, つける ③(ある状態に)する ④putの過去, 過去分詞 **put down** 下に置く, 下ろす **put in** ~の中に入れる **put on** ~を…の上に置く **put out** 外に出す **put ~ into …** ~を…に突っ込む

Q

□ **queen** 名女王, 王妃

□ **question** 名質問, 疑問

□ **quickly** 副敏速に, 急いで

□ **quiet** 形 ①静かな, 穏やかな, じっとした ②おとなしい, 無口な, 目立たない 名静寂, 平穏 動静まる, 静める

□ **quietly** 副 ①静かに ②平穏に, 控えめに

R

□ **rabbit** 名うさぎ **White Rabbit** 白うさぎ

□ **race** 名競争, 競走

□ **racer** 名出場者, 競走者

□ **ran** 動run(走る)の過去

□ **read** 動読む, 読書する **read out** 読み上げる

□ **reading** 名読書, 読み物, 朗読

□ **ready** 形用意[準備]ができた, まさに~しようとする, 今にも~せんばかりの **be ready to** すぐに[いつでも] ~できる, ~する構えで

□ **real** 形実際の, 実在する, 本物の

□ **reality** 名現実, 実在, 真実(性)

□ **realize** 動理解する, 実現する

□ **really** 副本当に, 実際に, 確かに

□ **recite** 動暗唱する, 復唱する, 物語る, 朗読する

□ **red** 形赤い 名赤, 赤色

□ **refuse** 動拒絶する, 断る

□ **relieved** 形安心した, ほっとした

□ **remember** 動思い出す, 覚えている, 忘れないでいる

□ **rest** 動①休む, 眠る ②休止する, 静止する ③(～の)ままである **rest on** ～の上に載っている

□ **return** 動帰る, 戻る, 返す

□ **right** 形①正しい ②適切な 副①まっすぐに, すぐに ②ちょうど, 正確に

□ **river** 名川

□ **rock** 名岩, 岩石

□ **Rome** 名ローマ《イタリアの首都》

□ **room** 名①部屋 ②空間, 余地

□ **rose** 名バラ(の花)

□ **rule** 名規則, ルール

□ **run** 動①走る ②運行する ③(川が)流れる ④経営する **run after** ～を追いかける **run away** 走り去る, 逃げ出す **run by** 走り過ぎる **run down** 駆け下りる **run in** 走って入る **run off** 走り去る, 逃げ去る **run out of a house** 家から外に走り出る

□ **rush** 動突進する, せき立てる **rush out of** 急いで～から出てくる **rush toward** ～に向かって突進する

S

□ **sad** 形①悲しい, 悲しげな ②惨めな, 不運な

□ **sadly** 副悲しそうに, 不幸にも

□ **safe** 形①安全な, 危険のない ②用心深い, 慎重な **keep ～ safe** ～を保護する **safe to drink** 飲んでも安全である

□ **said** 動say(言う)の過去, 過去分詞

□ **sang** 動sing(歌う)の過去

□ **sat** 動sit(座る)の過去, 過去分詞

□ **saw** 動see(見る)の過去

□ **say** 動言う, 口に出す

□ **school** 名学校

□ **scream** 動叫ぶ, 金切り声を出す

□ **sea** 名海

□ **seat** 名席, 座席

□ **second** 名(時間の)秒, 瞬時 **every second** 刻々と

□ **see** 動①見る, 見える, 見物する ②(～と)わかる, 認識する, 経験する ③会う ④考える, 確かめる, 調べる ⑤気をつける **see if** ～かどうかを確かめる

□ **seem** 動(～に)見える, (～のように)思われる **seem to be** ～であるように思われる

□ **seen** 動see(見る)の過去分詞

□ **send** 動①送る, 届ける ②手紙を出す ③(人を～に)行かせる ④《－＋人[物など]＋～ing》～を(ある状態に)する

□ **sense** 名①感覚, 感じ ②《-s》意識, 正気, 本性 ③常識, 分別, セ

ンス ④意味 **make much sense** 非常によくわかる **make sense** 意味をなす **make sense of** ～を解明する 動感じる, 気づく

☐ **sensible** 形 ①分別のある ②理にかなっている ③気づいている **in a sensible way** 良識ある態度で

☐ **sent** 動 send(送る)の過去, 過去分詞

☐ **servant** 名 召使, 使用人, しもべ

☐ **set** 動 ①置く, 当てる, つける ②整える, 設定する ③setの過去, 過去分詞 **set off** 出発する 形 ①決められた, 固定した ②準備のできた

☐ **shake** 動 ①振る, 揺れる, 揺さぶる, 震える ②動揺させる

☐ **shall** 助 ①《Iが主語で》～するだろう, ～だろう ②《I以外が主語で》(…に)～させよう, (…は)～することになるだろう

☐ **shape** 名 形, 姿

☐ **share** 動 分配する, 共有する

☐ **she** 代 彼女は[が]

☐ **shore** 名 岸, 海岸, 陸

☐ **should** 助 ～すべきである, ～したほうがよい **should have done** ～すべきだった(のにしなかった)《仮定法》

☐ **shoulder** 名 肩

☐ **shout** 動 叫ぶ, 大声で言う, どなりつける

☐ **shrink** 動 縮む, 縮小する

☐ **side** 名 側, 横, そば, 斜面 **one side** 片側

☐ **sight** 名 光景, 眺め

☐ **sign** 名 表示

☐ **silence** 間 Silence! 静かに!

☐ **silently** 副 静かに, 黙って

☐ **simple** 形 単純な, 簡単な, 質素な

☐ **sing** 動 (歌を)歌う

☐ **sir** 名 あなた, 先生《目上の男性, 客などに対する呼びかけ》

☐ **sister** 名 姉妹, 姉, 妹

☐ **sit** 動 座る, 腰掛ける **sit on** ～の上に乗る

☐ **six** 名 6(の数字), 6人[個] 形 6の, 6人[個]の

☐ **size** 名 大きさ, 寸法, サイズ

☐ **sleeping** 形 眠っている

☐ **sleepy** 形 ①眠い, 眠そうな ②活気のない **get sleepy** 眠くなる

☐ **slowly** 副 遅く, ゆっくり

☐ **small** 形 ①小さい, 少ない ②取るに足りない **get smaller** 小さくなる 副 小さく, 細かく

☐ **smile** 名 微笑, ほほえみ

☐ **smoke** 動 喫煙する, 煙を出す 名 煙, 煙状のもの

☐ **snail** 名 カタツムリ

☐ **sneeze** 動 くしゃみをする

☐ **so** 副 ①とても ②同様に, ～もまた ③《先行する句・節の代用》そのように, そう **so ～ that …** 非常に～なので… 接 ①だから, それで ②では, さて

☐ **some** 形 ①いくつかの, 多少の ②ある, 誰か, 何か **spend some time** いくらかの時間を割く[かける] **take some time** いくらか時間

がかかる 副約, およそ 代①いくつか ②ある人[物]たち

□ **somebody** 代誰か, ある人 **somebody else** 誰か他の人

□ **someone** 代ある人, 誰か

□ **something** 代①ある物, 何か ②いくぶん, 多少

□ **sometimes** 副時々, 時たま

□ **song** 名歌

□ **soon** 副まもなく, すぐに, すみやかに **as soon as** ～するとすぐ, ～するや否や

□ **sorry** 形気の毒に[申し訳なく]思う, 残念な

□ **sound** 動①音がする, 鳴る ②(～のように)思われる, (～と)聞こえる **sound like** ～のように聞こえる

□ **soup** 名スープ

□ **speak** 動話す, 言う, 演説する

□ **speaker** 名話す人, 演説者

□ **speaking** 動speak (話す)の現在分詞 名話すこと, 談話, 演説

□ **spend** 動①(金などを)使う, 消費[浪費]する ②(>時を)過ごす **spend some time** いくらかの時間を割く[かける]

□ **spent** 動spend (使う)の過去, 過去分詞

□ **spoke** 動speak (話す)の過去

□ **square** 名正方形, 四角い広場, (市外の)一区画

□ **stand** 動立つ, 立たせる, 立っている, ある **stand up** 立ち上がる

□ **start** 動①出発する, 始まる, 始める ②生じる, 生じさせる **start doing** ～し始める **start to do** ～し始める

□ **stay** 動①とどまる, 泊まる, 滞在する ②持続する, (～の)ままでいる

□ **steal** 動①盗む ②こっそりと手に入れる, こっそりと～する

□ **step** 名歩み, 1歩(の距離)

□ **still** 副①まだ, 今でも ②それでも(なお)

□ **stole** 動steal (盗む)の過去

□ **stone** 名石, 小石

□ **stood** 動stand (立つ)の過去, 過去分詞

□ **stop** 動①やめる, やめさせる, 止める, 止まる ②立ち止まる **stop doing** ～するのをやめる

□ **story** 名物語, 話

□ **straight** 副一直線に, まっすぐに, 垂直に **fall straight down** まっすぐに落ちる

□ **strange** 形①知らない, 見[聞き]慣れない ②奇妙な, 変わった

□ **strong** 形強い, 堅固な

□ **stuck** 動stick (刺さる)の過去, 過去分詞 形行き詰った, 動きがとれない

□ **study** 動勉強する, 研究する

□ **subject** 名学科

□ **such** 形①そのような, このような ②そんなに, とても, 非常に **such a** そのような

□ **suddenly** 副突然, 急に

□ **suggest** 動①提案する ②示唆する

□ **summer** 名 夏

□ **sun** 名《the –》太陽，日

□ **supposed** 形《be – to》～しなければならない，～することになっている

□ **sure** 形 確かな，確実な，《be – to ～》必ず［きっと］～する，確信して **make sure** 確かめる，確認する

□ **surprise** 動 驚かす，不意に襲う 名 驚き，不意打ち **to one's surprise** ～が驚いたことに

□ **surprised** 動 surprise（驚かす）の過去，過去分詞 形 驚いた

□ **surprising** 形 驚くべき，意外な

□ **surround** 動 囲む，包囲する

□ **swam** 動 swim（泳ぐ）の過去

□ **sweet** 名《-s》甘い菓子

□ **swim** 動 泳ぐ

T

□ **table** 名 テーブル，食卓，台

□ **tail** 名 尾，しっぽ

□ **take** 動 ①取る，持つ ②持って［連れて］いく，捕らえる ③乗る ④（時間・労力を）費やす，必要とする ⑤（ある動作を）する ⑥飲む ⑦耐える，受け入れる **take a bite** 一口かじる **take a break** 中断する **take notes** 記録を取る **take out** 取り出す **take out of** ～から出す **take some time** いくらか時間がかかる **take turns** 交代でする **take up**（時間・場所を）とる，占める **take ～ out of one's pocket** ポケットから～を取り出す **take ～ to …** ～を…に連れて行く

□ **talk** 動 話す，語る，相談する

□ **tall** 形 高い，背の高い **three inches tall** 身長3インチ

□ **tart** 名 タルト《菓子》

□ **taste** 動 味がする，味わう

□ **taught** 動 teach（教える）の過去，過去分詞

□ **tea** 名 茶，紅茶

□ **teacup** 名 ティーカップ

□ **tear** 名 涙

□ **tell** 動 ①話す，言う，語る ②教える，知らせる，伝える ③わかる，見分ける

□ **terrible** 形 恐ろしい，ひどい，ものすごい，つらい

□ **than** 接 ～よりも，～以上に **more than** ～以上

□ **thank** 動 感謝する，礼を言う **thank ～ for** ～に対して礼を言う

□ **that** 形 その，あの **that way** その方向に 代 ①それ，あれ，その［あの］人［物］ ②《関係代名詞》～である… 接 ～ということ，～なので，～だから **so ～ that …** 非常に～なので…

□ **the** 冠 ①その，あの ②《形容詞の前で》～な人々 副《– ＋比較級，– ＋比較級》～すればするほど…

□ **their** 代 彼（女）らの，それらの

□ **them** 代 彼（女）らを［に］，それらを［に］

□ **then** 副 その時（に・は），それから，次に **just then** ちょうどその時

□ **there** 副 ①そこに［で・の］，そこへ，あそこへ ②《– is［are］～》～がある［いる］ **here and there** あちこ

ちで

□ **these** 形 これらの，この

□ **they** 代 ①彼（女）らは[が]，それらは[が] ②（一般の）人々は[が]

□ **thin** 形 薄い，細い，やせた

□ **thing** 名 ①物，事 ②《-s》事情，事柄 ③《one's -s》持ち物，身の回り品 ④人，やつ **old thing** 旧友《英俗》

□ **think** 動 思う，考える **think to oneself** 心の中で思う

□ **thirteen** 名 13（の数字），13人[個] 形 13の，13人[個]の

□ **thirty** 名 30（の数字），30人[個] 形 30の，30人[個]の

□ **this** 形 ①この，こちらの，これを ②今の，現在の 代 ①これ，この人[物] ②今，ここ **at this** これを見て，そこで（すぐに）

□ **those** 形 それらの，あれらの 代 それら[あれら]の人[物]

□ **thought** 動 think（思う）の過去，過去分詞 名 考え，意見

□ **three** 名 3（の数字），3人[個] 形 3の，3人[個]の

□ **threw** 動 throw（投げる）の過去

□ **through** 前 ～を通して，～中を[に]，～中 副 ①通して ②終わりまで，まったく，すっかり **come through** 通り抜ける，通り過ぎる **fit through the door** ドアを通り抜ける **get through** ～を通り抜ける **go through** 通り抜ける **look through** ～をのぞき込む

□ **throw** 動 投げる，浴びせる，ひっかける **throw ~ at** ～を…に投げつける

□ **time** 名 ①時，時間，歳月 ②時期 ③期間 ④時代 ⑤回，倍 **any time** いつでも **at the time** そのころ，当時は **by the time** ～する時までに **spend some time** いくらかの時間を割く[かける] **take some time** いくらか時間がかかる

□ **tired** 形 ①疲れた，くたびれた ②あきた，うんざりした **get tired** 疲れる，飽きが来る

□ **to** 前 ①《方向・変化》～へ，～に，～の方へ ②《程度・時間》～まで ③《適合・付加・所属》～に ④《 ‒ ＋動詞の原形》～するために[の]，～する，～すること **to one's surprise** ～が驚いたことに

□ **today** 名 今日

□ **told** 動 tell（話す）の過去，過去分詞

□ **too** 副 ①～も（また） ②あまりに～すぎる，とても～ **too much** 過度の

□ **took** 動 take（取る）の過去

□ **top** 名 頂上，首位 **on top of** ～の上（部）に

□ **tortoise** 名 カメ（亀）

□ **toward** 前 ①《運動の方向・位置》～の方へ，～に向かって ②《目的》～のために **rush toward** ～に向かって突進する

□ **tree** 名 木，樹木

□ **trial** 名 裁判

□ **trouble** 名 ①困難，迷惑 ②心配，苦労 ③もめごと **in trouble** 困難な状態で

□ **try** 動 ①やってみる，試みる ②努力する，努める **try on** 試してみる

try out 試してみる

□ **turn** 動 ①ひっくり返す, 回転する［させる］, 曲がる, 曲げる, 向かう, 向ける ②（～に）なる,（～に）変える **turn around** 振り向く, 向きを変える, 方向転換する **turn into** ～に変わる［変化する］ **turn to** ～の方を向く 名 ①回転, 曲がり ②順番 ③変化, 転換 **take turns** 交代でする

□ **turtle** 名 ウミガメ（海亀） **Mock Turtle** にせウミガメ

□ **twelve** 名 12（の数字）, 12人［個］ 形 12の, 12人［個］の

□ **two** 名 2（の数字）, 2人［個］ 形 2の, 2人［個］の

U

□ **uglification** 名 醜化《造語》

□ **uglify** 動 醜くする

□ **under** 前 ①《位置》～の下［に］ ②《状態》～で, ～を受けて, ～のもと ③《数量》～以下［未満］の, ～より下の

□ **understand** 動 理解する, わかる, ～を聞いて知っている

□ **until** 接 ～の時まで, ～するまで

□ **up** 副 ①上へ, 上がって, 北へ ②立って, 近づいて ③向上して, 増して 前 ①～の上（の方）へ, 高い方へ ②（道）に沿って **come up to** ～のすぐそばまでやってくる **fill up**（穴・すき間を）いっぱいに満たす, 詰める **fill up with** ～でいっぱいになる **get up** 立ち上がる **grow up** 成長する, 大人になる **grown up** 成長した **jump up** 急に立ち上がる **look up** 見上げる **pick up** 拾い上げる, 手に入れる **stand up** 立ち上がる **take up**（時間・場所を）とる, 占める **wake up** 起きる, 目を覚ます

□ **us** 代 私たちを［に］ **let us** どうか私たちに～させてください

□ **used** 動《－to》よく～したものだ, 以前は～であった

□ **useful** 形 役に立つ, 有効な, 有益な

□ **usual** 形 通常の, いつもの, 平常の, 普通の

V

□ **vanish** 動 姿を消す, 消える, ゼロになる

□ **very** 副 とても, 非常に, まったく

□ **voice** 名 ①声, 音声 ②意見, 発言権

W

□ **wait** 動 ①待つ,《－for ～》～を待つ ②延ばす, 延ばせる, 遅らせる ③《－on［upon］～》～に仕える, 給仕をする

□ **wake** 動 ①目がさめる, 起きる, 起こす ②奮起する **wake up** 起きる, 目を覚ます

□ **walk** 動 歩く, 歩かせる, 散歩する **walk away** 立ち去る, 遠ざかる

□ **want** 動 ほしい, 望む, ～したい, ～してほしい **want to be** ～の状態でありたいと思う

□ **was** 動《beの第1・第3人称単数現在am, isの過去》～であった,（～

に）いた［あった］

□ **washing** 名洗濯

□ **watch** 名腕時計

□ **water** 名 ①水 ②（川・湖・海などの）多量の水

□ **way** 名 ①道，通り道 ②方向，距離 ③方法，手段 ④習慣 **in a sensible way** 良識ある態度で **that way** その方向に **way out** 出口 **way out of** ～から抜け出る道 **way to** ～する方法

□ **we** 代私たちは［が］

□ **well** 副 ①うまく，上手に ②十分に，よく，かなり **as well** 同様に 形健康な，適当な，申し分ない **as well as** ～と同様に 間へえ，まあ，ええと

□ **went** 動 go（行く）の過去

□ **were** 動《beの2人称単数・複数の過去》～であった，（～に）いた［あった］ **I wish ~ were** … 私が～なら …なのに。《仮定法過去》

□ **what** 代 ①何が［を・に］ ②《関係代名詞》～するところのもの［こと］ 形 ①何の，どんな ②なんと ③～するだけの 副いかに，どれほど

□ **when** 副 ①いつ ②《関係副詞》～するところの，～するとその時，～するとき 接 ～の時，～するとき 代いつ

□ **whenever** 接 ①～するときはいつでも，～するたびに ②いつ～しても

□ **where** 副 ①どこに［で］ ②《関係副詞》～するところの，そしてそこで，～するところ 接 ～なところに［へ］，～するところに［へ］ 代 ①どこ，どの点 ②～するところの

□ **which** 形 ①どちらの，どの，どれでも ②どんな～でも，そしてこの 代 ①どちら，どれ，どの人［物］ ②《関係代名詞》～するところの

□ **while** 接 ①～の間（に），～する間（に） ②一方，～なのに 名しばらくの間，一定の時 **after a while** しばらくして（から）

□ **white** 形 ①白い，（顔色などが）青ざめた ②白人の 名白，白色

□ **White Rabbit** 白うさぎ

□ **whiting** 名ホワイティング《タラ科の食用魚》

□ **who** 代 ①誰が［は］，どの人 ②《関係代名詞》～するところの（人）

□ **whole** 形全体の，すべての，完全な

□ **why** 副 ①なぜ，どうして ②《関係副詞》～するところの（理由） 間 ①おや，まあ ②もちろん，なんだって ③ええと

□ **wide** 形幅の広い，広範囲の，幅が～ある 副広く，大きく開いて

□ **will** 助 ～だろう，～しよう，する（つもりだ） **will have done** ～してしまっているだろう《未来完了形》

□ **win** 動勝つ，獲得する，達する

□ **window** 名窓，窓ガラス

□ **wish** 動望む，願う，（～であればよいと）思う **I wish I hadn't done** ～しなければよかったのに（してしまった） **I wish ~ were** … 私が～なら …なのに。《仮定法過去》

□ **with** 前 ①《同伴・付随・所属》

～と一緒に，～を身につけて，～とともに ②《様態》～(の状態)で，～して ③《手段・道具》～で，～を使って **off with** (すばやく) ～を取り去る **with all** ～がありながら **with fear** 怖がって

□ **witness** 名 目撃者，証人

□ **won** 動 win (勝つ)の過去，過去分詞

□ **wonder** 動 ①不思議に思う，(～に)驚く ②(～かしらと)思う **wonder if** ～ではないかと思う

□ **wonderful** 形 驚くべき，すばらしい，すてきな

□ **wonderland** 名 おとぎの国，不思議の国，すばらしい場所[土地]

□ **wood** 名《しばしば-s》森，林

□ **word** 名 ①語，単語 ②ひと言

□ **worried** 動 worry (悩む)の過去，過去分詞 形 心配そうな，不安げな

□ **worry** 動 悩む，悩ませる，心配する[させる]

□ **would** 助《willの過去》①～するだろう，～するつもりだ ②～したものだ **Would you like ～?** ～はいかがですか。 **would like to** ～したいと思う

□ **write** 動 書く，手紙を書く

□ **writing** 名 書くこと，作文，著述

□ **written** 動 write (書く)の過去分詞

□ **wrong** 形 間違った

Y

□ **yell** 動 大声をあげる，わめく

□ **yes** 副 はい，そうです 名 肯定の言葉[返事]

□ **yesterday** 名 ①昨日 ②過ぎし日，昨今 副 昨日(は)

□ **yet** 副 ①《否定文で》まだ～(ない[しない]) ②《疑問文で》もう ③《肯定文で》まだ，今もなお

□ **you** 代 ①あなた(方)は[が]，あなた(方)を[に] ②(一般に)人は

□ **young** 形 若い，幼い，青年の

□ **your** 代 あなた(方)の

ステップラダー・シリーズ
不思議の国のアリス

2021年10月4日　第1刷発行

原著者　ルイス・キャロル

発行者　浦　晋亮

発行所　IBCパブリッシング株式会社
〒162-0804 東京都新宿区中里町29番3号 菱秀神楽坂ビル9F
Tel. 03-3513-4511　Fax. 03-3513-4512
www.ibcpub.co.jp

印　刷　株式会社シナノパブリッシングプレス
装　幀　久保頼三郎
イラスト　長崎祐子　ジョン・テニエル(p.1)
リライト　ニーナ・ウェグナー
ナレーション　ケイティ・アドラー
録音スタジオ　株式会社巧芸創作

ISBN978-4-7946-0680-8